STIR FRY RECIPES

Easy Stir Fry Recipes for Very Easy Stir Fry Cooking

(An Easy Stir Fry Cookbook Everyone Loves!)

Dwight Deitz

Published by Sharon Lohan

Stir Fry Recipes: Easy Stir Fry Recipes for Very Easy Stir Fry Cooking (An Easy Stir Fry Cookbook Everyone Loves!)

ISBN 978-1-990334-50-4

Legal & Disclaimer

The information contained in this book is not designed to replace or take the place of any form of medicine or professional medical advice. The information in this book has been provided for educational and entertainment purposes only.

Table of contents

Part 1

Introduction

Stir frying is a Chinese cooking technique with centuries of history that has spread throughout the kitchens of the world. The wok, the Chinese frying pan typically used to stir fry, is thought to have been originally created to dry grain. Its shape was improved throughout centuries until it reached its current shape during the Ming dynasty, when it started to be used to fry in hot oil, or stir fry.

Who doesn't get watery mouths from smelling stir fry food? One of the most efficient tricks that Chinese people use to have their restaurants always full with costumers is to drop some vegetables in hot oil and toss the wok vigorously to spread the aroma throughout the street, like a magic enchantment. Apart from the hypnotizing smell, the true magic about stir fry dishes is mainly in the fact that stir frying adds so much richness to the flavors while preserving the colors and textures of the ingredients.

If you think that stir fry food is unhealthy, think again. Since the amount of oil used is extremely low, stir fry dishes usually are very low in fat while very rich in fresh vegetables and healthy grains. Also, it is a very simple and quick cooking method, so it is ideal for those of you who don't have much time or skills to dedicate to the kitchen. The most important thing to prepare a good stir fry dish is to be prepared with all of the ingredients before start cooking. Once the wok is hot, everything goes smoothly and fast until you end up with a bowl full of goodness.

In this vegan stir fry recipe book you can find 50 incredibly delicious and easy to make stir fry recipes that will help you prepare delicious meals within no time. These recipes are divided in six categories: Stir Fried Vegetables, Stir Fried Rice, Stir Fried Noodles, Tofu Stir Fry, Mushroom Stir Fry, and Quinoa Stir Fry. Try all recipes and enjoy the richness of flavors and textures of stir fry food at the comfort of your kitchen.

Stir Fried Vegetables

Vegetable Teriyaki Stir Fry

Teriyaki derives teri, that refers to a luster given by the sugar content of the sauce, and yaki, which refers to grilling or broiling as a cooking method. Teriyaki sauce adds a delicious taste to stir fry vegetables and leave them with a shining and irresistible look. Serve this stir fry on top of rice noodles, quinoa or brown rice.

Yields: Makes 2 servings.

Ingredients:
For the Sauce:
1/3 cup Tamari
¼ cup Water
3 tbsp Agave Nectar
1 tbsp freshly squeezed Lemon Juice
1 1/2 tsp toasted Sesame Oil
1 tsp Blackstrap Molasses
5 medium cloves Garlic, minced
2 tsp freshly grated Ginger
1 tbsp Tapioca Starch

For the Stir Fry:
½ tbsp Sesame Oil
5 cups Broccoli
Pinch of Sea Salt

2 tsp Water
1½ cups Yellow Bell Pepper, sliced
½ cup raw Cashews
½ cup Green Onions, sliced

Method of Preparation:
1. In a large mixing bowl, combine all the sauce ingredients, whisking together to fully incorporate the tapioca starch.
2. Prepare broccoli by cutting into flowerets and removing the stalks.
3. Add ½ tsp of sesame oil to a large non adherent skillet and heat it over high heat.
4. Add in the broccoli and a pinch of sea salt and a tsp of water. Toss it to cover and let it cook for about 2 to 3 minutes.
5. As the broccoli starts get a brighter green color add in the chopped bell pepper and let it fry for another minute.
6. Pour in the Teriyaki sauce and turn heat to high. Stir the mixture to coat the vegetables with sauce and let it come to a slow boil.
7. Once the sauce has thickened a bit, add in cashews and green onions. Stir through the sauce and remove from the heat. Serve immediately.

Chickpea & Snap Pea Stir Fry

Chickpeas and Snap Peas married together in this vegetable stir fry to provide you a healthy and nutritious dish that is satisfying and rich. It requires the preparation of a simple sauce that gives the dish moist and lust. Since most of the canned chickpeas have salt you don't need to add any, unless you like the food more on the salty side.

Yields: Makes 2 servings.

Ingredients:
1 can 15 oz can Chickpeas, rinsed and drained
2 cups Snap Peas
1 can 8 oz Water Chestnuts, sliced
1 pck 8 oz Button Mushrooms, sliced
1 pck 12 oz Broccoli florets
1 cup Carrots, sliced
1 small Red Bell Pepper, sliced
1 tbsp Olive Oil

For the Sauce:
½ cup Vegetable Broth
2/3 cup Soy Sauce
1/3 cup Rice Vinegar
2 tbsp Cornstarch
1 tbsp Brown Sugar
1 tsp finely grated Ginger
2 tsp Garlic Powder

1 tsp Sesame Oil

Method of Preparation:
To make the sauce:
1. In a medium mixing bowl, whisk together soy sauce, vegetable broth, rice vinegar, brown sugar, sesame oil, garlic powder, grated ginger and cornstarch. Stir to dissolve the sugar and reserve.

To make the stir fry:
2. Heat olive oil in a large skillet or wok over high heat. When hot, add in broccoli florets, sliced carrots, sliced mushrooms, snap peas and chopped pepper. Allow to cook for about 5 minutes stirring frequently.
3. When vegetables are tender crispy stir in the water chestnuts and drained chickpeas. Mix to incorporate and let it cook for about 1 minute.
4. Pour in the prepared sauce and toss to coat the vegetables with sauce. Continue cooking until the sauce thickens.
5. Remove skillet from heat and transfer stir fry to a serving bowl. Serve with brown rice or quinoa.

Lentil Almond Mint Stir Fry

This Lentil Almond Mint Stir Fry is the ideal dish to a warm and cozy dinner at the comfort of your home. It is earthy and filling and the mint sauce adds it freshness and soul. Avoid starch potatoes for this dish to keep it crunchy. You don't want a mashed potato texture here. The almonds and dates bring sweetness and richness to the dish, leaving a good taste in your mouth.

Yields: Makes 2 servings.

Ingredients:
8 very small new Potatoes, halved
1 can 15 oz Brown Lentils, drained
12 Brussels Sprouts, trimmed and quartered
2 Medjool Dates, pitted and chopped
¼ cup sliced Almonds, toasted
1 tbsp extra-virgin Olive Oil

For the Mint Sauce:
1 cup fresh Mint Leaves
½ Serrano Chile Pepper, seeded
½ tsp Sugar
1 tbsp Lemon Juice
2 tbsp Olive Oil
Pinch of Sea Salt

Method of Preparation:

To make the mint sauce:
1. Put mint leaves, Serrano chili pepper, olive oil, sugar, lemon juice and salt into the food processor and pulse to break down mint leaves. Adjust salt if needed and set aside.

To make the stir fry:
2. Add olive oil to a large skillet or wok and heat it over medium heat. Add in the potatoes and a pinch of sea salt, cover the skillet and allow them to cook for 5 minutes.
3. When the potatoes are tender remove the lid and turn the heat to medium-high and stir frequently. Let the potatoes acquire a golden color (about 2 minutes).
4. Pour in the lentils and cook to heat through. Transfer potatoes and lentils to large plate, cover to keep warm and set aside.
5. Using the same pan, cook the Brussels sprouts on a splash of olive oil over medium heat until tender and caramelized (approximately 5 minutes).
6. Add in the reserved lentils and potatoes to the skillet again and the sliced almonds, reserving some to garnish. Toss to combine and remove from heat.
7. Transfer to a large plate or bowl, drizzle the mint sauce and sprinkle the remaining almonds and chopped dates on top. Serve hot.

Beetroot & Carrots Stir Fry

Beetroots and carrots star in this stir fry dish filling with color and earthy deep flavors. This stir fry is a very simple recipe that turns out incredibly satisfying and nutritious. It makes a complete meal when served over a bed of rice or you can prepare it as a side to any protein main dish. It has a very subtle curry taste that balances perfectly the earthiness and sweetness of the roots.

Yields: Makes 4-6 servings.

Ingredients:
2 cups grated Carrots
1 cup grated Beetroots
1 tbsp grated Coconut
½ cup Onions, finally chopped
2 Green Chilli, finally chopped
½ tsp Cumin Seeds
½ tsp Mustard Seeds
2 Curry Leaves
1 tbsp fresh Cilantro, chopped
1 tsp Sea Salt
1 cup Water
1 tbsp Olive Oil

Method of Preparation:
1. In a large skillet or wok heat olive oil over medium-low heat. When hot add in chopped onions, cumin

and mustard seeds and curry leaves and stir. Let it cook for 1 minute.

2. Add in grated carrots and beetroots and ¾ cup of water and toss to coat. Let it stir-fry for about 8 to 10 minutes until tender.

3. Add in the grated coconut and the last ¼ cup of water and mix. Let it fry for another 4 minutes or so, until everything is soft and most of the water has been absorbed.

4. Remove from heat and transfer to a serving platter. Sprinkle fresh cilantro on top and serve it with rice.

Vegetable Curry Stir Fry

Warm up yourself with this Vegetable Curry Stir Fry. This recipe is a perfect blend of the vegetable crunchiness with the warm and fragrant flavor of curry. This dish ends up smooth and not too spicy. It has beautiful colors that look and taste delicious over a bed of white basmati rice. Let the rice soak the moist and flavors from the stir fry for a minute before serving.

Yields: Makes 4 servings.

Ingredients:
5 tbsp Olive Oil, divided
18 oz Zucchini, quartered and sliced
1 ½ lbs Eggplant, chopped
1 Yellow Bell Pepper, chopped
1 Red Bell Peppers, chopped
½ cup minced Onion
2 tsp minced fresh Ginger
2 tsp minced fresh Garlic
1 can 8 oz Tomato Sauce
1 tbsp + 1 tsp Curry Paste
1 tsp ground Cumin
1 tsp ground Coriander
1 tsp Sea Salt, divided

Method of Preparation:
1. Add 3 tbsp of olive oil to a large non adherent skillet or wok and heat it over medium-high heat.

2. Add in minced onion, minced ginger and garlic and ½ tsp of sea salt. Stir and let it fry onions are transparent but not browned.

3. Place in chopped eggplant and toss. Let it cook until soft, stirring occasionally. Transfer cooked vegetables to separate bowl and cover.

4. Add the remaining olive oil to the skillet. When hot, add in chopped yellow and red peppers and the remaining ½ tsp of sea salt. Stir-fry the peppers until they get tender-crispy.

5. Add in zucchini slices and cook it while stirring for 2 minutes. Transfer to the previous bowl and keep it cover.

6. Turn the heat to low and pour the tomato sauce on the skillet along with the curry paste, ground coriander and cumin. Stir to incorporate and to dissolve the curry paste.

7. Place the reserved vegetables on the skillet and stir to coat with sauce. Let it incorporate the flavors for 1 final minute. Remove from heat and serve hot over basmati rice.

Baby Turnip & Spring Onions Stir Fry

Turnips are an underestimated root that should definitely be more present in our kitchens. They have a characteristic earthy flavor and a crunchy texture. Baby turnips are softer and more pleasant to taste and the greens are tender and rich. Use both to prepare this simple and delicious stir fry that matches perfectly with any grain.

Yields: Makes 3 servings.

Ingredients:
1 lb Baby Turnips, with greens
½ cup Spring Onions, sliced
¼ cup Vegetable Stock
1 tbsp Soy Sauce
1 tsp Agave Nectar
1 clove Garlic, minced
1 tbsp minced Ginger
Pinch of Sea Salt
Pinch of freshly ground Pepper
2 tbsp Canola Oil
½ cup fresh Cilantro, roughly chopped

Method of Preparation:
1. In a small mixing bowl whisk together soy sauce, vegetable stock and agave nectar and set aside.
2. Separate greens from turnips and chop roughly. Scrub baby turnips and cut them in 2 to 4 pieces.

3. Add 1 tbsp of oil to a large skillet or wok and heat it over high heat. Swirl the skillet to spread the oil and add in garlic and ginger. Stir-fry them for about 30 seconds.
4. Add in chopped spring onions and cook for 1 minute while stirring.
5. Add in chopped turnips and stir-fry them for about 2 minutes. Pour in the soy sauce and season with salt and pepper. Toss to distribute the flavors.
6. Add in turnip greens and fry them for another 1 to 2 minutes, until they get softened.
7. When all the veggies are tender crispy remove from heat and sprinkle the fresh cilantro. Toss to combine and transfer to a serving bowl.

Eggplant & Black Bean Stir Fry

This Eggplant & Black Bean Stir Fry is a very simple dish that you can put together in about 15 minutes with few ingredients. Serve it over a bead of basmati rice to have a complete and satisfying meal. Black beans are an easy-to-combine ingredient, you can also add any other vegetable that you have in the fridge. You can save some of the chopped green onion to sprinkle on top at the end.

Yields: Makes 4 servings.

Ingredients:
2 large Eggplants, sliced
1 can 15 oz Black Beans, drained
2 Red Bell Peppers, cut into thin strips
8 Spring Onions, finely sliced
½ tsp ground Cumin
2 tbsp Olive Oil
2 tbsp Water
Pinch of Sea Salt
Pinch of Black Pepper

Method of Preparation:
1. Heat a large skillet or wok over medium-high heat and add in the oil. When hot, add in the slices of eggplant and stir-fry for 10 to 12 minutes until soften and golden.

2. Add in the chopped spring onions and peppers and cook for another 6 minutes while stirring.
3. When the peppers are tender crispy pour in the black beans, 2 tbsp water and cumin. Toss to combine and let the beans heat through.
4. When hot, season with salt and pepper to taste and remove from heat. Serve with basmati rice.

Pumpkin Cashew Stir Fry

This simple Pumpkin Cashew Stir Fry is super easy to prepare and never disappoints. The pumpkin ends up tender crispy without getting too mushy. The cashews add the dish flavor, texture and protein. The sauce makes the stir fry shinning and appealing. This dish is comforting, colorful and super healthy, so you should give it a try.

Yields: Makes 4 servings.

Ingredients:
4 cups Pumpkin, chopped
¼ cup Cashews
2 cup Kale, roughly chopped
1 Onion, sliced thick
1 tsp minced Garlic
1 Red Chili, sliced
1 tbsp Olive Oil
2 tsp Soy Sauce
1 tsp Palm Sugar
½ cup Vegetable Stock

Method of Preparation:
1. Heat the oil in a wok or a skillet on medium-high heat. When hot, add in the chopped onion, minced garlic and chili. Let them stir-fry until the onions get transparent.

2. Add in the pumpkin and let it cook slightly brown on the edges but still firm.
3. Mix in chopped kale, cashews, palm sugar, soy sauce and vegetable stock. Stir to combine and let it cook until the sauce starts to reduce and thicken.
4. When the sauce has reduce to about half the volume remove from heat and serve immediately. Pair with rice or noodles.

Apple & Veggies Stir Fry With Orange Ginger Sauce

Add a fruity twist to your veggie stir fry with this one. This stir fry includes apples for a sweet touch and an orange ginger sauce that adds an exotic flavor. It may sound like a lot of fruit in just one dish but their sweetness doesn't get too overwhelming. Avoid overcooking the apples so they remain crunchy and do not turn into puree.

Yields: Makes 4 servings.

Ingredients:
1 cup Baby Spinach
1 cup Onion, sliced
1 cup Carrot, thinly sliced
1 cup Celery, sliced
2 Apples, sliced
1 tbsp Olive Oil

For the sauce:
½ cup freshly squeezed Orange Juice
2 tbsp Soy Sauce
2 tbsp Rice Vinegar
1 tbsp Orange Zest
2 cloves Garlic, minced
1 tsp grated fresh Ginger

Method of Preparation:

To make the sauce:

1. In a large mixing bowl, whisk together all the sauce ingredients and reserve

To make the stir fry:

2. Heat a wok or large skillet over medium-high heat and add in the olive oil. When hot add in the baby spinach and sliced carrots and let them cook until tender crispy (approximately 5 minutes).
3. Add in the chopped onion and celery and allow cooking for 5 minutes more, stirring frequently.
4. Pour in the prepared sauce and toss to incorporate. Let it cook for 2 to 3 minutes to reduce.
5. Add the apple slices and stir to coat in sauce. Cook for 2 to 3 minutes more and serve.

Pecan Broccoli Stir Fry

Stir Fry broccoli is definitely the easiest way to get to enjoy this super nutritious veggie. It stays crunchy and flavorful, with a nice lust that makes it so visually appealing. Here, broccoli florets are paired with pecans creating an interesting mixture of textures and flavors. The lemon juice and zest helps the flavors to come through and add freshness and vibrancy.

Yields: Makes 4 servings.

Ingredients:
3 lbs Broccoli, chopped
1 clove Garlic, minced
1/3 cup Pecans, roughly chopped
3 tbsp Olive Oil
1 Lemon, juice and zest
Pinch of Sea Salt
Pinch of ground Black Pepper

Method of Preparation:
1. Chop broccoli into small florets. Peel the stalk and shred it.
2. Heat the oil in a wok or skillet over medium-high heat. Add in garlic and pecans and let them fry for 1 minute while stirring.
3. Add in shredded broccoli stalk and florets and toss to coat with oil. Cover and let it cook for until

tender crispy (approximately 6 minutes), stirring occasionally.

4. Season to taste with salt and pepper. Pour in lemon juice and sprinkle with lemon zest. Stir to incorporate and remove from heat. Serve immediately.

Stir Fried Rice

Spring Fried Rice

This fried rice is so colorful and fresh that it will always remind you that spring has sprung. It is light, flavorful and makes a terrific garnish for veggie spring rolls and many other main dishes. You can use any long grain rice or basmati rice, if you prefer. Use tamari instead of soy sauce for a gluten-free version.

Yields: Makes 2 servings.

Ingredients:
1 cup Rice, long grain
1 Carrot, diced
½ cup Corn Kernels, fresh or frozen
½ cup Peas, fresh or frozen
½ Onion, chopped
2 cloves Garlic, minced
2 tbsp Soy Sauce
1 tbsp extra virgin Olive Oil
2 cups Water

Method of Preparation:
1. Cook 1 cup of rice in 2 cups of boiling water over low heat until al dente. Let it cool down to room temperature.

2. Cook peas and corn in boiling water until soft (approximately 15 minutes). Drain them and set aside.
3. Using a wok or skillet, heat olive oil over medium heat. When hot, add in chopped onion, minced garlic and diced carrots and cook them for about 2 minutes.
4. Add in cooked peas and corn kernels and let them fry for 2 about minutes while stirring.
5. Mix in the rice and pour soy sauce over it. Stir for another 2 or 3 minutes. Transfer to a serving bowl and serve.

Curry Stir Fried Rice

This Curry Stir Fried rice will make you travel to Asia from the first to the last bite. It is incredibly aromatized by a warm curry sauce that can be prepared in a few minutes. The ginger gives it freshness and the jalapeño a challenging hot touch. It makes a complete meal by itself since it is rich in vegetables, or it can be match with a protein main dish.

Yields: Makes 4-6 servings.

Ingredients:
1 ½ cup Basmati Rice
3 cups Water
2 cups Broccoli Florets
10 oz sliced Carrots
1 Red Bell Pepper, chopped
½ medium Onion, sliced
2 cloves Garlic, minced
1 tbsp fresh Ginger, grated
1 Jalapeño, chopped
2 tsp Cornstarch
1 cup Vegetable Broth
1 tbsp Soy Sauce
2 tsp Curry Powder
½ tsp Turmeric
¼ tsp Sea Salt
1 tbsp Canola Oil

Method of Preparation:

1. Cook basmati rice in boiling water over medium-low heat until all water has been absorbed. Set aside.
2. In a medium mixing bowl, whisk together vegetable broth, cornstarch, soy sauce, curry powder, turmeric and salt. Mix well and reserve.
3. Add canola oil to a wok or a large deep pan and heat it over medium-high heat. Add in ginger, onion and garlic and let it fry for one minute while stirring. Transfer to a bowl and reserve.
4. Put broccoli florets, carrots, red bell pepper and jalapeño into the hot pan and stir fry them for 2 to 3 minutes until crispy tender. Transfer to the previous bowl and reserve.
5. Whisk broth mixture once again and pour it into pan. Let it cook while stirring until sauce has thickened. Return all reserved vegetables to the pan and let them stir fry for an additional minute.
6. Add in cooked rice and stir. Let it absorb the flavors for 2 minutes while stirring.
7. Transfer to serving bowls and serve.

Cabbage Stir Fried Rice

Cabbage is an incredibly healthy vegetable that is available throughout the year. Napa or Savoy varieties work better in this recipe since their light texture will stir fry perfectly without being too hard. This recipe calls for a final touch of freshly squeezed lime juice that helps to wake up the flavors and make the dish more vibrant.

Yields: Makes 4 servings.

Ingredients:
1 ½ cups long grain white Rice
3 cups Water
4 cups Napa or Savoy cabbage, shredded
1 cup Carrots, finely sliced
1 small Yellow Onion, diced
2 tbsp fresh Ginger, peeled and minced
2 cloves Garlic, minced
2 tbsp Soy Sauce
Juice of 1 Lime
2 Scallions, finely sliced
2 tbsp Olive oil

Method of Preparation:
1. Cook rice in boiling water over low heat. Let all water be absorbed by the rice. Remove from heat and set aside.

2. In a wok or large skillet add in oil and heat it over medium-high heat. Add in onion, cabbage and carrots and stir-fry them over high heat until soft and slightly brown (approximately 5 minutes).
3. Add in garlic and ginger and toss. Let them cook for 1 minute until fragrant. Add in the rice and stir fry it until beginning to brown (approximately 3 minutes).
4. Remove the wok from the heat and mix in the lime juice, soy sauce and scallions. Transfer the serving bowls and enjoy.

Thai Pineapple Fried Rice

This Thai Pineapple Fried rice will cause sensation at your party. Serve it in a carved-out pineapple (use flesh to cook the rice) for an exotic presentation. Serving details apart, this rice is an explosion of flavors. The sweetness of the pineapple, raisins and cashews contrasts perfectly with the saltiness of the soy sauce. It is fragrant and colorful and both good served hot or cold.

Yields: Makes 4-6 servings.

Ingredients:
1 ½ cups long grain Rice
3 cups Water
1 ½ cups fresh Pineapple chunks
¼ cup Raisins
½ cup roasted Cashews
½ cup frozen Peas
¼ cup Vegetable broth
3 Spring Onions, finely sliced
2 Shallots, finely chopped
3 cloves Garlic, finely chopped
1 Red Chili, thinly sliced
1/3 cup fresh Coriander, chopped
2 tbsp Sesame Oil

For the Sauce:
2 tsp Curry Powder

3 tbsp Soy Sauce
½ tsp Sugar

Method of Preparation:
1. Cook rice in boiling water over low heat until all the water has been absorbed. Let it cool down completely.
2. Add 1 tbsp of oil to rice and mix it using your fingers. Separate any big chunks and reserve.
3. In a cup, whisk together the soy sauce and the curry powder and set aside.
4. Add 1 tbsp of oil into a wok or large frying pan and heat it over medium-high heat. Add in garlic, shallots, and chili. Let them stir fry for 1 minute until fragrant.
5. When the wok becomes dry, add in 1 tbsp of vegetable broth. Keep adding broth to keep ingredients frying, 1 tbsp at a time.
6. Add in peas and let them fry for 1 or 2 minutes. Keep adding stock when needed.
7. Add the rice, raisins, cashews and pineapple chunks and stir.
8. Pour in the soy sauce and curry mixture and mix gently to combine. Stop adding stock and let it fry for 5 to 8 minutes. Turn off heat and sprinkle the chopped coriander on top.
9. Remove from heat and serve by scooping rice onto a serving dish or in a carved out pineapple.

Wild Rice Veggie Stir Fry

Wild rice has a nice chewy texture and a nutty flavor that adds intensity to your veggie stir fry. It has a nice mixture of colors turning a simple dish into something that looks much more elaborated than it really is. Don't forget that wild rice takes longer to cook than regular rice and it will need a little bit more of water or vegetable stock too.

Yields: Makes 4-6 servings.

Ingredients:
2 cups Vegetable Stock
1 cup Wild Rice
¼ cup Sesame Oil
½ cup chopped Bok Choy
1 tbsp chopped Garlic
1 tbsp chopped fresh Ginger
¼ cup julienned Red Bell Pepper
¼ cup diced Poblano Chili
¼ cup Bean Sprouts
¼ cup chopped Scallions
2 tbsp Soy Sauce
2 tbsp chopped fresh cilantro
1 tsp fresh Lime Juice

Method of Preparation:
1. Combine wild rice and vegetable stock in a medium saucepan, cover it and cook the rice over medium-

low heat for approximately 40 to 50 minutes, until al dente. Reserve.

2. Add sesame oil to a wok and heat it over high heat. When hot, add chopped bok choy and stir-fry it for 1 minute while stirring.
3. Add in the minced garlic and ginger and cook them for 30 seconds.
4. Toss in the bell pepper, chili and scallions and let them fry for 2 minutes.
5. Stir in the cooked wild rice and stir to combine. Pour in the soy sauce, lime juice and cilantro. Remove from heat and serve immediately.

Sweet Soy Fried Rice

You will be amazed by the taste of this Sweet Soy Fried rice. The brown sugar and soy sauce adds a caramel-like feeling that is comforting and quite addictive. This recipe works best with long grain brown rice since it is chewer that white rice and has a mild nutty flavor that pairs perfectly with the sweet sauce. Finish the dish with fresh mint and basil to make it light and vibrant.

Yields: Makes 4 servings.

Ingredients:
1 ½ long grain brown Rice
4 cups Water
3 tbsp Peanut Oil, divided
2 cloves Garlic, minced
3 finely chopped Shallots
1 chopped Serrano Chile
1/3 cup fresh Cilantro, chopped
1/3 cup fresh Mint Leaves
1/3 cup fresh Basil Leaves
¼ tsp Sea Salt
¼ tsp ground Black Pepper
1 ½ cups Daikon Radish, thinly sliced
4 Lime Wedges

For the Sweet Soy Sauce
¼ cup low sodium Soy Sauce
¼ cup dark Brown Sugar

Method of Preparation:
1. Cook brown rice in boiling water over low heat until tender and set aside.
2. Heat 1 tbsp of oil in a wok or large skillet over medium-high heat and swirl to coat. Add in garlic, chili and shallots and stir-fry for about 1 or 2 minutes.
3. Add in cooked rice and mix well. Let it stir-fry for another 3 minutes.
4. In a small sauce pan whisk together soy sauce and brown sugar and bring to a boil over medium heat. Let it simmer for 2 minutes to reduce and thicken.
5. Pour the sweet soy sauce over the rice. Mix well and let rice absorb the flavors for 1 minute.
6. Season with salt and pepper and remove from heat.
7. Transfer rice to a serving platter and sprinkle sliced radish, chopped herbs and lime wedges and serve hot.

Stir Fried Risotto With Peas & Basil

The original risotto recipes require stir frying the rice in order to obtain the best results. The rice should get slightly transparent after the stir frying process. Then, the cooking goes smoothly and easy until it is al dente. It requires a close eye to keep adding the stock and avoiding that it dries. The result is a tender and chewy rice full of creaminess and soul.

Yields: Makes 4 servings.

Ingredients:
2 tbsp pure Olive Oil
1 medium Yellow Onion, chopped
1 cup Arborio rice
3½ cups Vegetable Broth
1 can 15 oz Peas, drained
1¾ tsp Sea Salt
¼ cup fresh Basil Leaves

Method of Preparation:
1. Add olive oil to a skillet or wok and heat it over medium heat. Add in chopped onion and stir-fry it until transparent and soft.
2. Add the rice and let it fry for 2 minutes while stirring. The grains should get translucent.
3. Add ½ cup of vegetable broth and stir. Let the rice cook and absorb almost all stock until adding the next scoop of stock, stirring occasionally.

4. When the rice is midway cooked, add in the drained peas and stir. Keep adding stock until the rice is cooked al dente.
5. Season with salt and fold in chopped fresh basil leaves.
6. Turn off the heat, cover the skillet and let it set for 2 minutes and then serve.

Peanut & Shiitake Glutinous Stir Fried Rice

Glutinous rice has a chewy texture and is steamed instead of boiled. It makes super comforting and filling stir fry dishes that are moist and flavorful. In this recipe, peanuts are added for their crunchy texture and sweet flavor that balances perfectly with the saltiness of the shiitake mushrooms and the creaminess of the rice.

Yields: Makes 6 servings.

Ingredients:
2 cups Long-grain Glutinous Rice
1 oz dried Shiitake Mushrooms
½ cup roasted Peanuts
3 Carrots, peeled and grated
1 tsp finely grated fresh Ginger
1 tbsp Sesame Oil
1 tbsp Olive Oil
3 tbsp Sweet Soy Sauce
1 tsp Sugar

Method of Preparation:
1. Place the rice in a bowl, cover with water and let it soak overnight.
2. Soak mushrooms in 1 cup of boiling water for 1 hour. After that, drain the mushrooms, saving the liquid for later, and finely chop them.

3. Add sesame oil to a skillet and heat it over medium heat. Add in chopped mushrooms and grated carrots and stir-fry them for about 5 minutes.
4. Add in peanuts and ginger and let them cook for another minute.
5. Combine soy sauce and sugar with 1 tbsp of mushroom water in bowl and stir to dissolve the sugar. Pour into the carrot mixture and stir to incorporate. Remove from heat and set aside.
6. Drain the rice and transfer to small dish that fits in the steamer. Mix in ¼ cup of water and place the rice in steamer. Let it steam for 25 to 30 minutes, until tender (add more water if necessary).
7. Transfer steamed rice to large bowl and mix in 1 tbsp of olive oil and the carrot mixture. Serve warm.

Stir Fry Noodles

Snow Pea Rice Noodle Stir Fry

Rice noodles are light, delicious and extremely easy to prepare. They only need to be soaked for a brief moment in hot water and they are ready to be mixed in a stir frying skillet with your favorite vegetables. Here snow peas are used along with asparagus to provide the dish some color and crunchiness, which contrasts perfectly with the softness of rice noodles.

Yields: Makes 4 servings.

Ingredients:
6 oz Rice Sticks or Rice Vermicelli
7 oz Snow Peas
1 cup Asparagus
3 cloves Garlic, minced
3 Green Onions, thinly sliced
¾ cup Vegetable Broth
2 tbsp low-sodium Soy Sauce
1 tsp toasted Sesame Oil, divided
¼ tsp White Pepper

Method of Preparation:
1. Put rice sticks into a large bowl and let them soak in hot water for about 8 minutes. Drain well and reserve.

2. Prepare snow peas and asparagus by slicing them lengthwise into ½ - 1 inch pieces.
3. Add 1 tsp of sesame oil to a non-adherent skillet and heat it over medium-high heat.
4. Add in asparagus and snow peas and stir-fry them for 3 to 4 minutes.
5. Toss in garlic and cook it for 1 minute while stirring.
6. Using a small mixing bowl, whisk together vegetable broth and soy sauce. Pour the mixture into pan and bring to a simmer.
7. Add in rice sticks and mix well. Let them cook for another 3 to 5 minutes to absorb the liquid.
8. Mix in chopped green onions and let them cook for another 2 to 3 minutes. Remove from heat and serve.

Thai Stir Fry Noodles

This simple Thai Stir Fry is made with a fresh sauce that gives aroma and interest to the noodles. Use wheat noodles or rice noodles for a gluten-free dish. It is important to cook the noodles al dente so they keep a nice texture when mixed in the stir fry. The bean sprouts add crunchiness and intensity to the dish and the fresh basil finish the dish with freshness and color.

Yields: Makes 3-4 servings.

Ingredients:
6 oz Wheat or Rice Noodles
6 Shiitake mushrooms, sliced
2 cups Bean Sprouts
1 small head Broccoli, chopped into florets
1 Carrot, sliced
¼ cup Purple Onion, chopped
1 small Yellow Bell Pepper, sliced
4 cloves Garlic, minced
2 tsp fresh Ginger, grated
2 tbsp fresh Basil, roughly chopped
2-3 tbsp Sesame Oil

For the Thai Sauce:
3 tbsp Soy Sauce
2 tsp Brown Sugar
3 tbsp fresh Lime Juice
3 tbsp Rice Vinegar

¼ tbsp White Pepper
¾ tsp Chili Flakes

Method of Preparation:
To make the Thai sauce:
1. Put all the sauce ingredients in a small mixing bowl and stir well until the sugar has dissolved. Reserve.

To make the stir fry:
2. Cook noodles in boiling water with a pinch of sea salt until al dente. Drain the noodles and rinse them with cold water and set aside.
3. Add sesame oil into a large frying pan or wok and heat it over medium-high heat. When hot swirl around and stir-fry the garlic, ginger and onion for 1 minute.
4. Add in the carrot slices and 1 to 2 tbsp of the prepared Thai sauce. Toss and let it fry for 2 minutes, until carrots start to get soft.
5. Add in the chopped mushrooms, broccoli florets and yellow pepper along with 3 or 4 more tbsp of sauce. Let it stir-fry until the mushrooms and the yellow pepper start to soften and broccoli florets get a bright green (approximately 3-4 minutes).
6. Add in the cooked noodles along with the remaining Thai sauce. Toss the noodles to coat and combine. Stir-fry for the last 3 to 5 minutes, adding the bean sprouts during the last minute.
7. Remove from heat and serve immediately in serving bowls or dishes, and sprinkle with fresh basil.

Cauliflower Peanut Stir Fry Noodles

This Cauliflower Peanut Stir Fry Noodles recipe is dedicated to the peanut butter addicts out there. Once you taste it you will not be able to stop. Peanut butter is the soul of this dish, giving it sweetness and moisture. The cauliflower ends up with a nice crunchy texture and the final sprinkle of roasted peanuts and fresh thyme leaves is just perfection over perfection.

Yields: Makes 4 servings.

Ingredients:
1 pck Rice Noodles
1 cup Cauliflower, chopped into florets
1/3 cup unsalted Peanut Butter
1 cup shredded Carrots
4 stalks Celery, chopped
4 Green Onions, chopped
1 tsp Red Pepper Flakes
1/4 cup fresh Orange Juice
1/4 cup Soy Sauce
1 tbsp roasted Peanuts
4 stalks fresh Thyme
1 tbsp Olive Oil

Method of Preparation:

1. Cook the rice noodles in boiling water for 4 to 5 minutes over medium heat. Drain the noodles and reserve them covered to keep them warm.
2. In a small mixing bowl, prepare the sauce by mixing together orange juice, soy sauce, peanut butter and red pepper flakes and reserve for later.
3. Add olive oil to a large skillet or wok and heat it over medium-high heat. Add in the carrots, celery, cauliflower florets and green onions and stir-fry them until they start to soften (approximately 5 to 7 minutes).
4. Pour in the prepared sauce and toss to coat. Let it cook for another 4 to 5 minutes.
5. Add in the noodles and stir gently to incorporate. Stir-fry one last minute to heat through and remove from heat.
6. Transfer to serving bowls or dishes and sprinkle roasted peanuts and fresh thyme leaves on top. Serve while hot.

Roasted Asparagus & Sun-Dried Tomatoes Noodle Stir Fry

This stir fry includes roasted asparagus and sun-dried tomatoes for rich experience of textures and flavors. Asparagus are very fibrous and are generally difficult to cook by only stir frying them. By roasting in the oven before adding them to the stir fry, they get tender and easier to digest, without losing their crispiness.

Yields: Makes 3 servings.

Ingredients:
1 pck rice Noodles
1 can 15 oz Chickpeas
1 lb Asparagus, hard ends cut off
4 Sun-dried Tomatoes, soaked and sliced in strips
1 tbsp Olive Oil + drizzle
2 cloves Garlic, grated
½ tsp Red Pepper Flakes
½ Lemon, juiced
Pinch of Sea Salt

Method of Preparation:
1. Put rice noodles in a small pan and cover with water. Cook for 4 to 5 minutes over medium heat. Drain the noodles and reserve them covered to keep them warm.

2. Preheat oven to 450 F. Chop asparagus into 1 ½ inch pieces and place them in a roasting pan. Add a drizzle of olive oil and sprinkle with grated garlic and sea salt. Let them roast for about 10 minutes until slightly tender. Remove from oven and set aside.
3. Heat 1 tbsp of olive oil in a wok or skillet over medium-high heat. When hot, place in chopped sun-dried tomatoes and chickpeas. Toss to coat and fry for 2 minutes.
4. Add in the noodles and the roasted asparagus and stir to combine. Season with salt and red pepper flakes and pour in the lemon juice. Mix to incorporate and let it fry for another minute while stirring.
5. Remove from heat and serve hot in a large bowl.

Veggie Stir Fry Noodle Soup

This Veggie Stir Fry Noodle Soup is the perfect recipe for those cold winter evenings. Get warm and cozy and enjoy a bowl full of goodness that is prepared in a blink of an eye. This soup is light, comforting and rich in warm flavors. Stir fry veggies end up crunchy, contrasting perfectly with the softness of the noodles. You can prepare it with wheat noodles too.

Yields: Makes 3 servings.

Ingredients:
2 cups Vegetable Stock
1 pck Rice Noodles
½ cup Carrots, sliced
1 can 8 oz Peas
½ cup Broccoli florets
½ tsp grated fresh Ginger
1 clove Garlic, minced
1 tsp Soy Sauce
1 tbsp Olive Oil
Pinch of Sea Salt
1 tbsp fresh Cilantro, chopped

Method of Preparation:
1. Add olive oil to a wok and heat it over medium-high heat. Add in minced garlic and ginger and let them fry for about 1 minute, stirring occasionally.

2. Add in carrots and broccoli florets and stir-fry for 5 minutes, until tender crispy.
3. Meanwhile, pour vegetable stock into a pan and bring to a boil. Add in rice noodles and cook them for 5 minutes. Cover to keep hot and reserve.
4. Add drained peas to the wok and toss to combine. Let them fry for another 2 minutes.
5. Pour in soy sauce and season with salt.
6. Transfer the stir fry mixture to the pan containing noodles and stock and stir to combine.
7. Pour into soup bowls, sprinkle with fresh cilantro and serve hot.

Veggie Kelp Noodle Stir Fry

Kelp noodles are made from a brown seaweed (kelp), sodium alginate and water. They are vegan, gluten-free and very low in calories. They can be served raw in salads or stir fried with veggies. This recipe conjugates them perfectly with some fresh veggies to make a light and colorful dish that is fun and interesting.

Yields: Makes 2 servings.

Ingredients:
12 oz Kelp Noodles
1 cup Baby Bok Choy, chopped
½ Red Bell Pepper, sliced
¼ cup Bean Sprouts
3 medium Spring Onions, sliced
1 tbsp Soy Sauce
1 ½ tbsp Sesame Oil
3 cloves Garlic, crushed
1 tsp fresh Ginger, grated
Pinch of Sea Salt

Method of Preparation:
1. Rinse kelp noodles and set aside.
2. Add sesame oil to a large skillet or wok and heat it over medium-high heat. Add in chopped baby bok choi and red bell pepper and stir-fry for about two minutes, until tender crispy.

3. Add in spring onions and cook for about 1 minute, stirring frequently.
4. Add in garlic and ginger and toss to release the flavors.
5. When all veggies are tender crispy, pour in soy sauce and season with salt. Toss to combine. Finally, add in bean sprouts and stir for about 20 seconds.
6. Turn off the heat and incorporate the kelp noodles. Serve immediately.

Curry Udon Noodle Stir Fry

Udon noodles are Japanese wheat flour and are thicker than rice noodles. They make delicious stir fry dishes and soups that are filling, comforting and rich. This Curry Udon Noodle Stir Fry is a good example of how these noodles can be applied. This dish requires the preparation of an easy curry roux that adds creaminess and richness to the stir fry.

Yields: Makes 2-3 servings.

Ingredients:
1/2 pound fresh Udon Noodles
4 tbsp Canola Oil
2 tbsp All-purpose Flour
1 ½ tsp Curry Powder
½ tsp Garam Masala
¾ cup Vegetable Broth
2 tsp Sugar
1 large Yellow Onion, sliced thinly
1 tsp fresh Ginger, grated
1 Red Bell Pepper, thinly sliced
1 Hot Red Chili, stem and seeds off and thinly sliced
½ lb Broccoli florets, chopped
3 tbsp Soy Sauce

Method of Preparation:

1. Bring a pot of water to a boil. Cook the udon noodles covered in boiling water for about 10 to 12 minutes. Drain and reserve.
7. Add 2 tbsp of the oil in a medium saucepan and heat it over medium-low heat. Add in the flour and stir well. Let it cook until brown roux (about 10 minutes).
8. Add in the garam masala and curry powder, mix well and cook for one more minute.
9. Slowly pour in ½ cup of the vegetable stock, while whisking.
10. Add in the sugar and continue cooking until it thickens. Turn off the heat and reserve.
11. Pour the remaining 2 tbsp of oil into a large skillet and heat over medium heat. Add in chopped onion and cook until transparent.
12. Add in the ginger, hot red chili and red bell pepper. Stir and cook for about 5 minutes. Add in the broccoli florets and stir-fry until tender crispy (4 to 5 minutes).
13. Mix in the udon noodles and cook for another minute. Pour in the soy sauce and toss to coat. Cook for another minute.
14. Pour in the prepared curry roux and the remaining vegetable broth and stir well to coat. Allow cooking for a last minute to warm up and serve immediately.

Veggie Stir Fry Noodle Salad

If you avoid salads because you always feel hungry and unsatisfied afterwards you might want to give this one a try. This Veggie Stir Fry Noodle Salad is vibrant, healthy and very satisfying. It combines fresh greens with cooked noodles and stir fry veggies in perfect harmony of flavors and textures. It is light, flavorful and very rich and comforting.

Yields: Makes 6 servings.

Ingredients:
1 pck Rice Noodles
1 pck 16 oz Baby Greens
2 Red Bell Peppers, finely sliced
1 cup Spring Onions, finely sliced
2 Carrots, sliced
8 Kaffir Lime Leaves
½ cup Bean Sprouts
2 tbsp Sesame Oil
1 tbsp grated fresh Ginger
2 cloves Garlic, finely chopped
3 tbsp Soy Sauce
2 tbsp Sesame Oil
2 tbsp fresh Cilantro, chopped

For the Dressing:
¼ Rice Vinegar
2 sticks Lemongrass

1/3 fresh Red chili
2 tbsp Golden Caster Sugar

Method of Preparation:
To make the dressing:
1. Place all sauce ingredients and 4 of the kaffir lime leaves in a small saucepan. Bring to a simmer and allow boiling for 1 minute. Remove from the heat and let it set.

To make the salad:
2. Cook the noodles in boiling water for about 5 minutes. Drain and reserve covered.
3. Add 2 tbsp of the sesame oil to a wok or skillet and heat it over medium heat. Add in the carrots, peppers, garlic and ginger and stir-fry them for about 1 minute.
4. Add in spring onions and cook for 3 minutes stirring frequently. Pour in soy sauce and toss to combine. Remove from heat and fold in bean sprouts.
5. Shred the other 4 lime leaves and fold them in the stir-fry mixture.
6. Toss the cooked noodles into a bowl and pour the dressing over them. Stir to coat.
7. Place the baby greens on big serving platter and pour the noodles over them. Top with the stir fry veggies and a sprinkle of chopped fresh cilantro and serve.

Tofu Stir Fry

Tofu & Broccoli Stir Fry

While extremely good for you, broccoli might not be the easiest veggie to fall in love with. If not cooked right it might have a funny smell and not so interesting texture. However, well-cooked broccoli is surprisingly good and has a nice crunchy texture. This recipe will help turn your plain broccoli florets into delicious crunchy and juicy bites.

Yields: Makes 2 servings.

Ingredients:
1 pck 14 oz extra-firm Tofu
6 cups Broccoli florets
½ cup Vegetable Broth
1 tbsp minced Garlic
1 tbsp minced fresh Ginger
2 tbsp Lemon Juice
1 tsp Apple Cider Vinegar
3 tbsp low sodium Soy Sauce
2 tbsp + 1 tsp Sugar
3 tbsp Cornstarch, divided
14 tsp ground Red Pepper
1/4 tsp Sea Salt
3 tbsp Water
2 tbsp Canola Oil, divided

Method of Preparation:
1. In a small mixing bowl, whisk together vegetable broth, lemon juice, vinegar, soy sauce, 1 tbsp of cornstarch, ground red pepper and sugar. Set aside.
2. Drain tofu and cut it into cubes with about ¾ inch. Sprinkle with sea salt.
3. Put 2 tbsp of cornstarch in a large mixing bowl and toss the tofu cubes in it to coat.
4. Add 1 tbsp of oil to a large non adherent skillet or wok and heat it over medium-high heat.
5. Add in the tofu and let it cook until brown (approximately 3 minutes) without stirring.
6. Gently turn the tofu and let the other side to cook while stirring occasionally. Let it get a brown color all over (2 to 3 minutes more). Transfer the tofu to a plate and set aside.
7. Reduce heat to medium and add the remaining tbsp of oil. When hot add in garlic and ginger and cook them until fragrant (approximately 30 seconds).
8. Add in broccoli florets and water. Cover the skillet or wok and let it cook until tender and crispy while stirring occasionally (2 to 4 minutes).
9. Pour in the broth mixture and let it cook for 1 to 2 minutes to thicken.
10. Add in the tofu and stir to combine. Transfer stir fry to a serving bowl or plate and serve hot.

Eggplant & Tofu Pesto Stir Fry With Couscous

Pesto is a traditional Italian sauce which acquired its name from the traditional crushing method of the garlic and the basil leaves in olive oil with a mortar and pestle. Most of us now use a food processor to make it easier and faster. However, the truth is that the old crushing method helped the flavors to come through better. If you have a mortar and pestle try it and you'll note the difference.

Yields: Makes 2 servings.

Ingredients:
1 tbsp Balsamic Vinegar
2 cloves Garlic, minced
2 pck firm Tofu, drained and cubed
1 + 1/3 cup Vegetable Stock
1 cup Couscous
2 tsp extra virgin Olive Oil
1 large Red Onion, cut into thin wedges
3 baby Eggplant, thinly sliced diagonally
2 green Zucchini, thinly sliced diagonally

For the Pesto:
2 tbsp Pine Nuts
1 cup fresh Basil Leaves
¼ cup Vegetable Stock
3 tsp extra virgin Olive Oil
2 clove Garlic, crushed

Pinch of Sea Salt
Pinch of freshly ground Black Pepper

Method of Preparation:
To make the pesto:
1. Toast pine nuts for 1 to 2 minutes in a small saucepan over medium heat. Remove from heat and transfer to the food processor.
2. Add in stock, olive oil, salt, pepper and crushed garlic to the food processor. Pulse to process until smooth, scraping down the walls when needed. Alternatively, crush everything using a mortar and pestle.
3. Transfer the pesto to a bowl and cover it with film. Reserve.

To make the stir fry:
4. In a large glass mixing bowl, combine 1 tbsp of pesto with balsamic vinegar and minced garlic.
5. Add in cubed tofu and toss to coat. Cover the bowl with film and let it marinate for 30 minutes to absorb the flavors.
6. Put 1 cup of vegetable stock in a small saucepan and bring it to a boil over high heat.
7. Remove stock from heat and add in the couscous. Use a fork to mix in the couscous and cover. Let the couscous absorb the stock (approximately 5 minutes).

8. After all the stock has been absorbed by the couscous, use a fork to lose the grains. Cover again and set aside.
9. Heat 1 tsp of olive oil in a large wok or skillet over medium-high heat. Add in the tofu cubes and let it fry for about 5 minutes until lightly browned. Transfer fried tofu to the pesto marinade bowl and stir to coat. Reserve.
10. Heat another tsp of olive oil in the wok or skillet over medium-high heat and stir-fry the onion for 3 minutes.
11. Add in the eggplant slices and let it fry for approximately 3 minutes, stirring occasionally.
12. Add in zucchini slices and stir-fry for about 2 minutes.
13. Pour in the extra 1/3 cup of vegetable stock and let it cook for 2 minutes while stirring.
14. When the vegetables are tender add in tofu and pesto marinade and mix. Let it stir-fry for another minute to heat through.
15. Scoop couscous into serving bowls and top with the stir-fry. Drizzle the remaining the pesto on top and serve.

Tofu & Cashews Stir Fry

Cashews are a delicious nut that add a sweet and comforting touch to your tofu stir fry dishes. This recipe has a perfect balance of spice and sweetness from the chili, ginger and tamarind sauce. It is rich in protein from the tofu, cashews and soy beans and the Pak Choi cabbage adds an interesting crunchiness and the needed fiber to balance the dish.

Yields: Makes 4 servings.

Ingredients:
2 pck firm Tofu, cubed
½ cup roasted Cashews
1 cup Spring Onions, sliced
1 can 15 oz Soy Beans
2 heads Pak Choi Cabbage, roughly sliced
4 cloves Garlic cloves, sliced
1 Red Chili, deseeded and finely sliced
1 tbsp Sesame Oil
1 ½ tbsp Tamarind Sauce
1 tbsp low-salt Soy Sauce

Method of Preparation:
1. Put the sesame oil in a non-adherent wok or skillet and heat it over medium-high heat.
2. Add in the garlic and chili and let them fry for about 30 seconds to 1 minute.

3. Mix in the spring onions, soy beans, sliced cabbage and tofu cubes. Let it stir-fry for 2 to 3 minutes.
4. Pour in tamarind and soy sauces and toss to coat. Fold in roasted cashews and let it fry for 2 minutes more while stirring.
5. Remove from heat and serve it by itself or over white rice.

Apple & Cranberry Tofu Stir Fry

This Apple & Cranberry Tofu Stir Fry in rich in flavor and textures. The apples and cranberries add it a juicy and fruity touch without turning the stir fry too sweet. The balsamic vinegar gives it a shining luster and a desired acidity. Serve it over brown rice or pasta. The leftovers reheat perfectly the following day.

Yields: Makes 2 servings.

Ingredients:
2 cups firm Tofu, cubed
2 Gala apples, chopped with skin
¼ cup dried Cranberries
1 tbsp Olive oil
4 Roma Tomatoes, chopped
¼ cup Chives, chopped
½ cup White Onion, chopped
2 tbsp Balsamic vinegar

Method of Preparation:
1. In a large skillet or wok, add the olive oil and let it become hot over medium heat.
2. Add in chopped apple, chopped tomatoes, cubed tofu, and chopped onion. Let them stir fry while tossing occasionally.
3. When tofu begins to get a light brown color (approximately 4 to 5 minutes), add in chopped chives and dried cranberries. Stir to combine and

reduce heat to low. Let it cook for another 2 to 3 minutes.

4. Pour in the balsamic vinegar and toss to combine for 30 seconds.
5. Remove skillet from heat and serve immediately.

Dried Tofu Stir Fry

Drying the tofu before stir frying it will take to other level of eating tofu. Dried tofu is more porous and has a tougher texture, making it more prone to absorb delicious flavors while frying. The process is quite simple, you only need to drain it between towels and then bake it at high temperature in the oven. It may sound like a laborious process but the result it totally worth it.

Yields: Makes 2 servings.

Ingredients:
For the Stir Fry:
1 pck 14 oz firm or extra firm tofu
1 cup Carrots, diced
2 cups Green Beans, roughly chopped
2 tbsp toasted Sesame Oil

For the Sauce:
1 tbsp fresh grated Ginger
1 tbsp Cornstarch
2 tbsp Brown Sugar
1 tbsp Maple Syrup
1/4 cup Soy Sauce

Method of Preparation:
To dry the tofu:

6. Preheat oven to 400 F and prepare a baking sheet with parchment paper.
7. Remove the tofu from the package and put it between towels. Place a heavy pan on top of it and let it drain for 15 minutes or so. After well drained, chop tofu into cubes with approximately 1 inch.
8. Spread tofu cubes on the prepared baking sheet and bake in the preheated oven for 25 to 35 minutes, tossing occasionally to ensure cooking all sides. Once golden brown and firm, remove from the oven and reserve.

To make the stir fry:
9. Put all sauce ingredients in a small mixing bowl and whisk well. Set aside.
10.Add sesame oil to a large skillet and heat it over medium heat. Add in the veggies and stir to coat. Cook them for 5 to 7 minutes, while stirring.
11.When the vegetables have softened, pour in the sauce and mix well. Let it thicken a bit.
12.Add in the dried tofu and mix. Let it cook for another 3 to 5 minutes while stirring.
13.When everything is cooked remove from heat and serve immediately.

Tempeh And Brussels Sprouts Stir Fry

This is a super easy and rapid dish to prepare. It makes a very satisfying meal on its own but it can be garnished with cook rice too. Instead of tempeh, it can also be prepared with tofu or a grain as protein source, if you prefer so. The leftovers can be kept in the fridge and re-heated. Actually, the flavors intensify with time, so you may find you like it even better the following day.

Yields: Makes 2 servings.

Ingredients:
1 pck plain Tempeh
2 cups fresh Brussels Sprouts
2 medium Carrots
1 medium Red Bell Pepper
1 cup Green Onions
2 tbsp grated fresh Ginger
3 cloves Garlic cloves
1 tbsp Cornstarch
2 tbsp Rice Vinegar
3 tbsp Soy Sauce
¼ cup Water
4 tbsp Sesame Oil

Method of Preparation:

5. In a small mixing bowl combine cornstarch with soy sauce, rice vinegar and water. Whisk well and reserve.

6. Wash, trim and cut the Brussels sprouts in halves and set aside. Cut the tempeh in cubes to a separate small bowl. Chop the green onions into another small bowl. Grate fresh ginger and mince garlic and reserve them together in another small bowl. Peel and slice carrots and seed and finely chop the bell pepper.

7. Heat 2 tbsp of sesame oil in a large frying pan or wok over high heat. Once oil is hot, add in the Brussels sprouts and let them cook for approximately 4 minutes, stirring occasionally to prevent burning.

8. Transfer the cooked Brussels sprouts to a medium bowl and reserve.

9. Wipe the pan with a paper towel and heat another tbsp of sesame oil on it. Add in cubed tempeh and cook while stirring until golden and start to get crispy (approximately 5 minutes).Reserve the cooked tempeh in the bowl that has the Brussels sprouts.

10.Wipe the pan once again and heat the last tbsp of sesame oil. Stir ginger, garlic and green onions for about one minute. Add in carrots and red bell pepper and cook for approximately 2 minutes while stirring frequently, until they are soft.

11.Pour in cooked Brussels sprouts and tempeh cubes and stir to combine the vegetables.

12. Whisk again the prepared sauce and pour over the vegetables. Let it thicken for about 2 minutes while stirring. Transfer to a serving bowl and serve.

Spinach & Sesame Tofu Stir Fry

This Spinach & Sesame Tofu Stir Fry is a very simple and fast recipe that makes a complete and nutritious meal. It is juicy and rich, ideal to serve over a bed of white rice, noodles or even as a filling for pita bread. The flavors are balanced, neither too spicy nor too plain, and the sesame seeds give the dish a final special touch.

Yields: Makes 2 servings.

Ingredients:
1 pck 12 oz Baby Spinach
½ lb Tofu, cubed
¼ tsp Red Chili Flakes
1 large clove Garlic, minced
1 tsp grated fresh Ginger
2 tbsp toasted Sesame Seeds
1 tbsp Canola Oil
1 tsp Soy Sauce
Pinch of Sea Salt
Pinch of ground Black Pepper

Method of Preparation:
1. Heat canola oil over medium-high heat in a large skillet or wok. When hot, add in tofu cubes and stir-fry them until the lightly colored (approximately 3 to 5 minutes).

2. Add in minced garlic and grated ginger and allow cooking until fragrant while stirring (about 1 minute).
3. Pour in soy sauce and mix. Add the baby spinach and stir-fry until it softens (about 1 to 2 minutes).
4. Fold in the sesame seeds and season with salt and pepper to taste. Remove from the heat and serve with rice or other grains.

Fried Tofu & Tomatoes Stir Fry

If you are a deep-fried tofu lover this is the stir fry for you. Tofu is deep-fried before stir frying with vine-ripened tomatoes to produce a rich and juicy stir fry. It is light, comforting and very moist. It serves perfectly over a big bed of pasta, since it has enough juices to coat it. If you're not into deep-fried tofu you can also just stir-fry it in the wok.

Yields: Makes 4 servings.

Ingredients:
4 cups Canola Oil, for frying
1 ¼ lb medium or firm Tofu, cubed
1 cup Yellow Onion, sliced
2 tsp minced Garlic
1 ½ lb Vine-ripened Tomatoes, cut into ¾ inch wedges
1 tbsp Rice Vinegar
½ cup Green Onions, chopped
1 tbsp Olive Oil
Pinch of Sea Salt

Method of Preparation:
1. Pour 4 cups of canola oil in deep pot and heat it to 375 F. Deep-fry the tofu cubes until they get a golden brown color. Stir gently so cubes don't stick to each other while frying. Drain tofu on paper towels and reserve.

2. Add 1 tbsp of olive oil to a wok or large skillet and heat it over high heat. When hot, add onion and garlic and cook them until onion gets transparent (about 1 to 2 minutes), stirring frequently.
3. Add in tomatoes and let them cook until tomatoes start to break down, stirring gently (about 1 to 2 minutes).
4. Pour in the rice vinegar and toss to combine. Add in the reserved tofu and green onions and stir to combine. Allow to fry for another minute and season with salt to taste.
5. When the tofu has warmed up turn off the heat and serve immediately.

Mushroom Stir Fry

Shiitake & Asparagus Stir Fry

Shiitake mushrooms are well known by their anticancer properties and high iron content. Their smooth texture cooks perfectly and rapidly in a hot wok, adding soul and tenderness to stir fry dishes. In this quick stir fry, crunchy asparagus contrast divinely with the meaty shiitake mushrooms turning it very satisfying and rich. Serve it over white or brown rice.

Yields: Makes 4-6 servings.

Ingredients:
6 oz Shiitake Mushrooms, stems removed and thinly sliced
1 lb Asparagus
2 tsp Sesame Seeds
1 tbsp fresh Ginger, peeled and grated
1 clove Garlic, minced
2 tbsp freshly squeezed Lemon Juice
¼ cup Vegetable Broth
1 ½ tbsp low-sodium Soy Sauce
3 tbsp Canola Oil

Method of Preparation:

1. Cut the asparagus lengthwise and into 2-inch pieces. Prepare mushrooms by removing stems and thinly slicing them.
2. Add sesame oil into a large fry pan and heat it over high heat. Add in minced garlic and grated ginger. Let it cook while stirring until fragrant (approximately 30 seconds).
3. Add in the mushrooms and cook them until brown, stirring constantly (about 2 minutes).
4. Mix in the asparagus and let them cook while stirring until they have a bright green color and a crisp-tender texture (approximately 3 minutes).
5. Pour in the lemon juice, vegetable broth and soy sauce and continue cooking until the liquid is reduced and thickened (approximately 2 to 3 minutes).
6. Mix in the sesame seeds. Remove from heat and transfer to a serving bowl or dish and serve immediately.

Portobello Mushroom & Eggplant Stir Fry

Portobello mushrooms, with their broad and flat scales, are ideal to serve stuffed with delicious stir fry veggies. The porous texture of eggplants easily absorbed the stir fry juices, creating a soft and flavorful stuff that contrasts perfectly with the tender flesh of the portobellos. In this simple stir fry recipe, few ingredients are needed to create a comforting and very satisfying dish.

Yields: Makes 2 servings.

Ingredients:
4 large Portobello Mushrooms, gills and stems removed
2 small Eggplants, sliced lengthwise and in strips
2 Green Onions, minced
½ cup Vegetable Broth
3 tbsp Soy Sauce
2 tbsp freshly squeezed Lemon Juice
1 tbsp Olive Oil + extra (to brush mushrooms)

Method of Preparation:
1. Heat olive oil over medium-high heat in a large non adherent skillet or wok.
2. Add in eggplant slices and stir-fry them until softened.

3. Add minced green onions and toss to combine. Let them cook for 2 minutes while stirring occasionally. Transfer mixture to a bowl and set aside.
4. Brush Portobello mushrooms with olive oil and place them in the hot skillet with the top side down. Reduce heat to medium and cover. Let it cook for 3 to 4 minutes and turn around to cook the other side for 3 minutes more.
5. When softened, remove mushrooms from skillet and reserve.
6. Turn the heat to high, pour in soy sauce and lemon juice and let it reduce a bit. Return reserved eggplant and mushrooms and stir-fry to heat through. Remove from heat.
7. To serve, place the Portobello mushrooms in a serving dish top down and stuff them with the eggplant mixture. Serve while hot.

Enoki Mushrooms With Spicy Green Beans Stir Fry

The long, thin and white Enoki mushrooms are the ideal type of mushroom if you are craving sea food. Their crispy texture makes delicious stir fry dishes, from which this one is a good example. Their pair up harmoniously with the sweet green beans and the spicy sauce adds the dish lots of character. Place the stir fry over a bed of white rice and let it set for a couple minutes before serving so the juiced turn the rice fragrant.

Yields: Makes 2 servings.

Ingredients:
½ lb fresh Enoki Mushrooms, root end trimmed
5 oz Green Beans, trimmed and sliced
4 cloves Garlic, finely minced
¼ tsp Chili Flakes
1 tsp Sugar
1 tsp Apple Cider Vinegar
2 tsp Sesame Oil
Pinch of Sea Salt

Method of Preparation:
1. In a small mixing bowl combine the garlic, the chili flakes, sugar and vinegar. Mix well to combine and reserve.

2. Add the sesame oil to a skillet or wok and heat it over medium-high heat.
3. When the oil is hot, add in the green beans and cook them for about 2 minutes, stirring frequently.
4. Add in the enoki mushrooms and let them stir-fry for about 1 minute while stirring, until they begin to soften.
5. Add in the sauce mixture and toss gently to coat the mushrooms. Let it reduce for another minute and remove from the heat.
6. Season with sea salt to taste and serve immediately over white rice or noodles.

Kale & Oyster Mushroom Stir Fry Salad

This Kale & Oyster Mushroom Stir Fry Salad is so addictive that you may run the risk of eating it while still in the skillet. The kale gets a tender texture and a vibrant green color that contrast beautifully with the light color of the oyster mushrooms. The mushrooms release a delicious savory juice while cooking that makes a rich natural dressing for the kale salad.

Yields: Makes 4 servings.

Ingredients:
1 tbsp Olive Oil
5 cloves Garlic, sliced
½ lb Oyster Mushrooms, bottom end trimmed
8 cups Kale, roughly chopped
Pinch of Sea Salt
Pinch of ground Black Pepper

Method of Preparation:
1. Add olive oil to a large non adherent pan and heat it over medium heat.
2. When the oil is hot, add in the garlic and let it cook until fragrant (approximately 1 one minute), stirring occasionally.
3. Add in the oyster mushrooms and stir-fry them for 5 minutes.

4. Place it the kale and toss to combine. Let it cook until the kale starts softened and gets a bright green color.
5. Turn off the heat and season with salt and black pepper. Transfer to a salad bowl and serve immediately.

Green Tomato & Cremini Mushroom Stir Fry

This Green Tomato & Cremini Mushroom Stir Fry is the perfect dish to prepare when you have too many green tomatoes sitting on the counter and you're not whiling to wait for them to get ripe. Their crunchy texture and tart flavor pair perfectly with the earthiness of the cremini mushrooms in this easy and fast stir fry.

Yields: Makes 2 servings.

Ingredients:
1 ½ tbsp Sesame Oil
2 cups Cremini Mushrooms, sliced
3 medium Green Tomatoes, sliced
½ tsp Cumin Seeds
¼ tsp Red Pepper Flakes
2 Hot Green Pepper, chopped
Pinch of Sea Salt
2 tbsp fresh Thyme, chopped
2 tbsp fresh Cilantro, chopped

Method of Preparation:
1. Wash the mushrooms and dry them with a paper towel. Slice them in 3 to 4 pieces each.
2. Add oil to a non-adherent skillet or wok and heat it over medium-high heat. When hot, add in the cumin seeds, chopped hot green peppers and pepper flakes.

3. When the cumin seeds start to sizzle, add in the chopped mushrooms and the sliced green tomatoes. Let them cook over high heat while stirring occasionally till the mushrooms softened and the juice evaporates.
4. Season with sea salt and turn off the heat. Transfer to a serving bowl or dish and sprinkle with fresh chopped thyme and cilantro and serve immediately.

Stir Fry Button Mushrooms With Rosemary & Shallots

This stir fry serves best on the dry side to let the caramelized shallots shine. To avoid having the mushrooms to sweet and release too much juice, it is important to cook them over high heat and let the skillet always uncovered. The rosemary and curry leaves add a beautiful fragrance to the dish. By the end you can either remove them or leave them for an extra crunchy touch.

Yields: Makes 2 servings.

Ingredients:
2 cups fresh Button Mushrooms
½ cup Shallots, peeled and sliced thin
5 cloves Garlic
1 Green Chili
1 spring Curry Leaves
3-5 springs Rosemary, roughly chopped
1 tbsp Coconut Oil
Pinch of Sea Salt
Pinch of freshly ground Black Pepper

Method of Preparation:
1. Rinse mushrooms gently in water and cut them into halves or four slices.

2. Heat a skillet or wok over medium-high heat. When hot pour in the coconut oil and let it heat.
3. Add in curry leaves and let them get crispy. Place in sliced shallots and let them fry for a minute.
4. Add in rosemary and sea salt and toss gently. Let it cook for another 2 minutes until the onions get a light pink color.
5. Add in the sliced mushrooms and stir-fry them over high heat for approximately 3 minutes.
6. Mince chili and garlic together and add them to the skillet. Mix to release the flavors and allow the mushrooms to cook completely (approximately 2 to 5 minutes more).
7. Turn off the heat and season with freshly ground black pepper to taste. Remove curry leaves and big rosemary springs if preferred and serve over toasted bread.

Mushroom & Veggie Stir Fry Soup

This Mushroom & Veggie Stir Fry Soup is pure decadence. It makes a golden and warm broth that it light and flavorful. It is a perfect appetizer for a dinner or even to serve in a party or get together. Slice the mushrooms finely or roughly according to your preferences. The soup works perfectly anyway.

Yields: Makes 4 servings.

Ingredients:
1 lb sliced Mushrooms, Cremini or Button
1 cup Carrot, finely chopped
1 cup Celery, finely chopped
1 cup Onion, finely chopped
1 clove Garlic, minced
1 cup Vegetable Broth
2 cups Water
¼ cup Tomato Paste
1 Bay Leaf
½ tsp ground Black Pepper
1 tbsp Rice Vinegar
1 tbsp Olive Oil

Method of Preparation:
1. Add olive oil to a wok or skillet and heat it over medium heat. Add in minced garlic and chopped onion and let them fry until onion is translucid. Keep stirring to avoid garlic to burn.

2. Add in chopped mushrooms, carrot and celery and stir-fry until mushrooms are soft (approximately 5 minutes).
3. Pour in tomato paste and toss to coat. Let it cook for 2 more minutes.
4. Transfer stir fry to a large pan and pour in vegetable stock, water, bay leaf and rice vinegar. Bring to a boil and reduce heat to low. Let it cook for 5 more minutes and serve hot.

Stir Fry Mushroom & Olive Tapenade

This Stir Fry Mushroom & Olive Tapenade is the perfect appetizer for your cocktails and parties. It is super rich and flavorful and spreads perfectly over crackers. Stirring the mushrooms with garlic adds soul to the tapenade, giving it a nice fragrance. Prefer high quality olives and olive oil for this recipe. Using fresh thyme is important too.

Yields: Makes 1 cup.

Ingredients:
1 cup Button Mushrooms, thinly sliced
1/3 + 1 tbsp Olive Oil
1 tbs Capers, drained and finely chopped
2 tbs chopped Chives
5 cloves Garlic, thinly sliced
¼ pitted Olives
1 Lemon, juiced
1 ½ tsp Sea Salt
½ tsp ground Black Pepper
4 stems of fresh Thyme

Method of Preparation:
1. Heat 1 tbsp of olive oil in a skillet over medium heat and add in 2 thinly sliced cloves of garlic. Let it fry for 1 minute while stirring.

2. Place in chopped mushrooms and cook for 5 to 6 minutes or until just tender. Remove from heat and drain excess moisture.
3. Transfer mushrooms to a food processor along with pitted olives, drained capers, fresh thyme and remaining cloves of garlic. Pulse to finely chop avoiding over processing.
4. Remove to a mixing bowl and pour in lemon juice, salt and pepper. Stir to incorporate and spoon into a cup or jar. Cover and place in the fridge for 30 minutes to cool down.
5. When cold, drizzle with extra virgin olive oil, sprinkle with chopped chives and serve with crackers.

Quinoa Stir Fry

Winter Veggie Quinoa Stir Fry

Veggie selection during winter may seem restrictive and boring. However, there are tons of delicious creations you can play with to give your winter veggie stash an exciting twist. This Winter Veggie Stir Fry recipe is a good example. Match your veggies with the protein-rich quinoa for a low-fat and gluten-free stir fry dish.

Yields: Makes 2 servings.

Ingredients:
1 cup Quinoa
2 cups Water
5 tbsp Olive Oil
2 cloves Garlic, finely chopped
3 Carrots, cut into thin sticks
1 medium Leek, sliced
1 cup Broccoli, cut into small florets
¼ cup Sundried Tomatoes, drained and chopped
1 cup Vegetable Stock
2 tsp Tomato puree
1 freshly squeezed Lemon

Method of Preparation:

1. Cook 1 cup of quinoa in 2 cups of boiling water for 15 to 18 minutes, adding more water if necessary.
2. Add 3 tbsp of olive oil to a wok or large skillet over medium heat.
3. Add in chopped garlic and let it fry for 1 minute, stirring constantly.
4. Add in the sliced carrots, chopped leek and broccoli florets. Let the vegetables fry for about 2 minutes, stirring often.
5. Toss in the sundried tomatoes and stir. In a small mixing bowl, whisk together the stock and tomato puree and pour it over the vegetables.
6. Cover the skillet and let it cook for 3 about minutes and turn off the heat.
7. Drain the quinoa and mix in remaining oil and lemon juice. Pour in warm plates and spoon the stir fried vegetables on top and serve immediately.

Asian Red Quinoa Stir Fry

Red quinoa makes colorful and interesting stir fry dishes and it only takes a few more minutes to cook than yellow quinoa. This Asian Red Quinoa Stir Fry recipe finishes with a tangy sauce of lime juice, tamarind and garlic that is soak by the quinoa giving it an interesting freshness. The vegetables end up tender but still crispy, contrasting perfectly with the cooked quinoa.

Yields: Makes 2 servings.

Ingredients:
1 cup dried Red Quinoa
1 tbsp Sesame Oil
1 small Red Onion, thinly sliced
1 clove Garlic, grated
1 tsp freshly grated Ginger, grated
½ tsp ground Coriander
1 tbsp Tamarind Sauce
1 Red Bell Pepper, sliced
1 large Zucchini, sliced with peel
½ cup fresh Green Beans, tailed and cut in half
2 tbsp Sesame Seeds
2 tbsp fresh Cilantro, roughly chopped
Water for cooking

For the Dressing:
2 Limes, zest and juice

½ clove Garlic, crushed
½ tsp Brown Rice Vinegar
1 tsp Tamarind Sauce
2 tbsp Sesame Oil
Pinch of Sea Salt

Method of Preparation:
To make the dressing:
1. Put all the dressing ingredients in a small mixing bowl and whisk until smooth and reserve.

To make the stir fry:
2. Cook red quinoa in boiling water for about 20 minutes until tender. Let it cool down to room temperature.
3. Pour sesame oil into a large skillet or wok and let it heat over medium-high heat.
4. Add in sliced red onion, grated garlic and ginger, ground coriander and tamarind sauce. Allow to fry for about 2 minutes.
5. Pour in 3 tbsp of water and stir. Let it fry for another minute and add in the bell pepper. Cook for 2 minutes more.
6. Add in more 4 tbsp water and let it reduce for 2 minutes. Add in the green beans along with ¼ cup of water and let it cook.
7. After 2 to 3 minutes, add in the zucchini and an additional ¼ cup of water and allow cooking for 3 more minutes. Turn off the heat and cover and reserve.

8. Mix the red quinoa into the veggie stir fry, add in the dressing and mix everything together. Sprinkle with the sesame seeds and the fresh cilantro and serve.

Golden Quinoa & Black Beans Stir Fry

This Golden Quinoa & Black Beans Stir Fry makes the meal by itself. It is comforting, complete and delicious. The black beans work better here than any other beans since their unique taste stands out and give character to the dish. For an extra fresh touch, drizzle a little of freshly squeezed lemon juice over it and enjoy it out of the stove.

Yields: Makes 2 servings.

Ingredients:
1 cup Golden Quinoa
2 cups Water
1 can 15 oz Black Beans
1 Shallot, chopped
2 tbsp Scallions, finely chopped
½ tsp fresh Ginger, grated
3 cloves Garlic, roughly chopped
1 tsp Chili Sauce
1 tsp Soy Sauce
1 tbsp Olive Oil
Pinch of Sea Salt
Pinch of ground Black Pepper

Method of Preparation:
1. Cook 1 cup of golden quinoa in 2 cups of boiling water for about 15 to 18 minutes until tender. Set aside.

2. Heat olive oil on a large skillet or wok over medium-high heat and add in shallots until they get lightly colored on edges (approximately 2 minutes).
3. Add in chopped garlic and grated ginger and allow cooking for about 1 minute, until fragrant.
4. Pour in the chili and soy sauces and mix. Add in cooked quinoa and toss to coat with sauce.
5. Drain beans and place them on the skillet and stir-fry for 3 to 4 minutes more.
6. Season to taste with sea salt and black pepper and sprinkle chopped scallions on top. Remove from heat and serve immediately.

Black Quinoa & Corn Stir Fry

This dish is colorful and fresh and very satiating. Black quinoa takes a couple more minutes to cook than the other quinoas but ends up as delicious as the others. This stir fry is made with the ingredients of a salsa sauce, which adds it flavor and soul. The final touch of the fresh cilantro and lime juice gives the dish freshness and fragrance.

Yields: Makes 2 servings.

Ingredients:
1 cup Black Quinoa
2 cups Water
1 can 15 oz Sweet Corn
1 ripe Tomato, chopped
1 small Onion, chopped
1 Red Bell Pepper, chopped
1 clove Garlic, minced
1 tsp Chili Powder
¼ cup fresh Cilantro, chopped
1 tbsp freshly squeezed Lime Juice
1 tbsp Olive Oil

Method of Preparation:
1. Cook 1 cup of black quinoa in 2 cups of boiling water for about 20 to 22 minutes. Add more water if necessary. Remove from heat when tender and set aside.

2. In a large skillet or wok heat olive oil over medium-high heat and add in minced garlic and chopped onion. Let it fry, stirring occasionally.
3. When onion is transparent add in chopped tomato and red bell pepper and let it fry until softened (approximately 3 to 4 minutes).
4. Drain corn and place it in the skillet. Stir to coat and let it stir-fry for about 3 minutes.
5. And in quinoa, chili powder and salt and pepper. Toss to combine and let it cook for 1 minute more to heat through, while stirring.
6. Remove from heat and transfer to a serving bowl. Sprinkle chopped cilantro on top and drizzle with lime juice. Serve immediately.

Spicy Red Cabbage Rainbow Quinoa Stir Fry

This Spicy Red Cabbage Rainbow Quinoa Stir Fry requires a few days of anticipation to ferment the spicy sauce. Alternatively you can by pre-made spicy sauce, such as Sriracha Sauce. Honestly, doing your own sauce will certainly give you extra satisfaction and you get to know exactly what's in it. The red cabbage and the rainbow quinoa make this dish colorful and crunchy.

Yields: Makes 4-6 servings.

Ingredients:
2 cups Rainbow Quinoa
4 cups Water
2 cups Red Cabbage
6 Scallions, chopped
1 cup Broccoli, chopped in florets
½ cup Carrots, diced
1 cup Pea Pods, chopped
4 cloves Garlic, minced
1 inch piece fresh Ginger, minced
2 tbsp Soy Sauce
1 tsp Sesame Oil

For the Spicy Sauce:
2 Red Jalapeño Peppers, stems cut off
1 Red Serrano Pepper, stem cut off
2 cloves Garlic
1 ½ tbsp Brown Sugar

1 tsp Sea Salt
1 tbsp Apple Cider Vinegar
3 tbsp Water

Method of Preparation:
To make the spicy sauce:
1. Chop peppers roughly keeping the seeds and process them in a food processor along with garlic, salt, brown sugar and water, until a smooth consistency is obtained.
2. Transfer sauce to a glass jar, cover with film and let it ferment in a cool dark place for 3 to 5 days protected from light. The sauce will start to bubble.
3. Pour the fermented sauce into the food processor and add in vinegar and blend until smooth. Strain it into a small saucepan, pressing the pulp. Discard seeds and skins.
4. Bring sauce to a boil and let it thicken for 5 to 10 minutes. Let it cool to room temperature and reserve. Keep leftovers in a airtight container in the fridge.

To make the stir fry:
5. Cook 2 cups of rainbow quinoa in 4 cups of boiling water for about 18 to 20 minutes. Add more water if necessary. Remove from heat when tender and reserve.
6. Heat a skillet or wok over medium-high heat and add in sesame oil. When hot, add the scallions, carrots, red cabbage, broccoli florets, pea pods,

garlic and ginger. Let everything cook together for 2 to 4 minutes until the veggies start to soften. Add in 1 or 2 tbsp of water if necessary.

7. Add in the cooked quinoa and stir-fry another 2 to 4 minutes, stirring frequently, until quinoa starts to get crispy.

8. Pour in the soy sauce and 2 tbsp of the prepared spicy sauce and stir to coat the veggies and quinoa for 1 more minute. Remove from heat and serve while hot.

Sweet Potato & Quinoa Stir Fry

This Sweet Potato & Quinoa Stir Fry is nutritious, satisfying and full of rich flavors. You can make it with your preferred quinoa but don't forget to adjust the cooking time to the chosen quinoa. Do not escape the final lime juice drizzle and lime zest since it add so much soul to the dish. Avoid overcooking the sweet potato so it doesn't get mashed in the stir fry.

Yields: Makes 2 servings.

Ingredients:
1 cup Quinoa
2 cup Water
1 8 oz Sweet Potatoes, peeled and cut into ½ inch cubes
2 tsp Canola Oil
½ cup Vegetable Broth
½ cup Onions, chopped
1 Red Bell Peppers, chopped
1 Jalapeño Pepper, finely chopped
2 cloves Garlic, minced
1 cup frozen Peas
1 tsp ground Cumin
¼ tsp Sea Salt
1/8 tsp ground Black Pepper
3 tbsp fresh Cilantro, chopped
1 Lime, juice and zest

Method of Preparation:

1. Cook 1 cup of quinoa in 2 cups of boiling water for about 15 (for yellow quinoa) to 20 minutes (if black quinoa). Add more water if necessary. Remove from heat when tender and reserve.
2. Chop all the vegetables, keeping them in separate bowls.
3. Put sweet potato cubes in another small saucepan and cover with cold water. Bring to a boil and let it cook until tender over medium-high heat (approximately 5 minutes). Drain the sweet potato and cover to keep warm.
4. Add canola oil to a large non adherent skillet or wok and heat it over medium-high heat.
5. Add in chopped onion and jalapeño pepper. Let them cook while stirring for 1 minute.
6. Add in chopped red bell pepper, minced garlic and ground cumin. Stir and continue cooking to soften the veggies (approximately 2 to 3 minutes).
7. Pour in ½ cup of vegetable broth and let it reduce for a couple minutes.
8. Add in peas and cook them for 2 minutes. Add in cooked quinoa and sweet potato cubes and stir gently to combine. Let it cook for 2 minutes to heat through and remove from heat.
9. Sprinkle fresh cilantro, sea salt, black pepper, lime juice and zest and serve immediately.

Quinoa Stir Fry Soup

Vegetable soups are like a magic passion that keeps cold and flu away. They are comforting, energizing and a natural boost to your defenses. Add a special touch to your veggie soup by using quinoa to make it more fulfilling and nutritious. This recipe will help with that.

Yields: Makes 6 servings.

Ingredients:
½ cup Quinoa
4 cups Vegetable broth
1 can 15 oz Red Kidney Beans, drained
1 can 28 oz crushed Tomatoes
 2 cups shredded Cabbage
½ cup diced carrot
½ cup chopped celery
1 onion, chopped
1 clove garlic, minced
2 tbsp olive oil
2 tbsp dried parsley
1 bay leaf
1 tsp dried basil
Pinch dried thyme

Method of Preparation:
1. Heat olive oil in a large pot over medium heat. Add in chopped onion, garlic and celery and diced carrot

and cook them until softened (approximately 5 to 10 minutes) while stirring frequently.

2. Add in parsley, basil, thyme, bay leaf, vegetable broth and tomatoes. Mix and bring to a boil. When it starts boiling reduce heat to low and let it cook for 10 minutes.

3. Stir in cabbage, quinoa and beans. Cover and let quinoa and cabbage cook until tender (approximately 18 minutes). Serve in bowls hot.

Quinoa & Black Bean Stir Fry Burgers

Who doesn't love homemade burgers served over soft bread buns? These Quinoa & Black Bean Stir Fry Burgers are a must try for all burger lovers out there. They are delicious and have a great burger-like texture that will not disappoint you. Quinoa and black beans are matched here to create the perfect crispy burger.

Yields: Makes 8 servings.

Ingredients:
½ cup Quinoa
1 ½ + 1 ½ cups Water
1 small Onion, finely chopped
6 oil-packed Sun-dried Tomatoes, drained and chopped
1 can 15 oz Black Beans, rinsed and drained, divided
2 cloves garlic, minced
Pinch of Sea Salt
Pinch of ground Black Pepper

Method of Preparation:
1. Cook quinoa in boiling water until tender (approximately 15 to 18 minutes).
2. Meanwhile, cook onion and drained sun-dried tomatoes in medium skillet heated over medium heat. Let them cook for 3 to 4 minutes until onion is transparent and soft.

3. Stir in the drained black beans, minced garlic and 1½ cups water. Cook for about 9 to 11 minutes and let most liquid to evaporate.
4. Transfer bean mixture to a food processor and add in ¾ cup of cooked quinoa. Pulse until smooth. Transfer the dough to a bowl and mix in remaining ¾ cup of cooked quinoa. Season with salt and pepper to taste and allow cooling down.
5. Preheat oven to 350 F and prepare greased baking sheet with cooking spray.
6. Shape bean-quinoa mixture into 8 burgers with hands and place them on the baking sheet. Allow to bake for about 20 minutes until the burgers get crispy on top. Flip the burgers over using a spatula and bake for another 10 minutes. Serve on bread buns.

Part 2

Anise Wine Chicken

Ingredients

1 small onion, chopped
2 inch piece fresh ginger root, minced
2 cloves garlic, minced
2 eaches whole star anise pods
1/2 cup dry white wine
1 teaspoon salt
1/4 teaspoon ground black pepper
2 tablespoons vegetable oil
1 teaspoon rice vinegar
1/2 pound skinless, boneless chicken breasts meat
- cut into bite-size pieces
20 eaches new potatoes
1 tablespoon vegetable oil
1 cup cherry tomatoes
1 tablespoon cornstarch
2 tablespoons water
1/4 cup minced fresh thai basil leaves

Directions

Step 1 Stir the onion, ginger, garlic, star anise, white wine, salt, pepper, 2 tablespoons vegetable oil, rice vinegar, and chicken together in a mixing bowl. Cover, and marinate in the refrigerator 4-6 hours. Meanwhile, place the potatoes in to a large pot and cover with salted water. Bring to a boil over temperature, then reduce heat to medium-low, cover, and simmer until tender, about quarter-hour. Drain and invite to cool before cutting in two.

Step 2 Heat 1 tablespoon of vegetable oil in a big skillet over high temperature. Get rid of the chicken from the marinade, and squeeze the surplus marinade from the chicken; reserve the marinade. Cook and stir the chicken in the hot oil until browned on all sides no more pink in the guts, about 5 minutes. Remove and discard the star anise from the marinade, and stir the marinade into the chicken. Bring to a boil, then add the cherry tomatoes and halved potatoes. Cook before potatoes are hot and the cherry tomatoes begin to burst, around 3 minutes. Dissolve the cornstarch in the water, and stir into the chicken mixture along with Thai basil. Cook and stir until thick, about 1 minute more.

Broccoli With Mandarin Oranges

Ingredients

2 (11-ounce) cans mandarin oranges, drained and liquid reserved
2 tablespoons molasses
1 tablespoon soy sauce
1/2 teaspoon ground ginger
1 1/2 teaspoons cornstarch
1/4 cup peanut oil
2 heads fresh broccoli, cut into florets
2 tablespoons sesame seeds

Directions

Step 1 In just a little bowl, mix together 1/4 cup of the reserved juice, molasses, soy sauce, ginger and cornstarch. Reserve.

Step 2 Heat oil in a wok over medium-high heat. Saute broccoli florets and you may of mandarin oranges before broccoli is heated through. The oranges will almost dissolve. Stir in the molasses mixture, and continue to cook while tossing the broccoli to coat before broccoli is tender, around 3 minutes.

Step 3 Remove from heat, and toss broccoli with all of those other can of oranges. Transfer to a serving plate, and sprinkle with sesame seeds.

Chicken With Basil Stir Fry

Ingredients

2 cups uncooked jasmine rice
1 quart water
3/4 cup coconut milk
3 tablespoons soy sauce
3 tablespoons rice wine vinegar
1 1/2 tablespoons fish sauces
3/4 teaspoon red pepper flakes
1 tablespoon olive oil
1 medium onion, sliced
2 tablespoons fresh ginger root, minced
3 cloves garlic, minced
2 pounds skinless, boneless chicken breasts halves - cut into 1/2 inch strips
3 mushrooms shiitake mushrooms, sliced
5 medium (4-1/8" long)s green onions, chopped
1 1/2 cups chopped fresh basil leaves

Directions
Step 1 Bring rice and water to a boil in a pot. Cover, reduce heat to low, and simmer 20 minutes.

Step 2 In a bowl, mix the coconut milk, soy sauce, rice wine vinegar, fish sauce, and red pepper flakes.

Step 3 In a skillet or wok, heat the oil over medium-high heat. Stir in the onion, ginger, and garlic, and cook until lightly browned. Mix in chicken strips, and cook around 3 minutes, until browned. Stir in the coconut milk sauce. Continue cooking until sauce is reduced be about 1/3. Mix in mushrooms, green onions, and basil, and cook until heated through. Serve over the cooked rice.

Chinese Pepper Steak

Ingredients

1 pound beef top sirloin steak
1/4 cup soy sauce
2 tablespoons white sugar
2 tablespoons cornstarch
1/2 teaspoon ground ginger
3 tablespoons vegetable oil, divided
1 red onion, cut into 1-inch squares
1 green bell pepper, cut into 1-inch squares
2 tomatoes tomatoes, cut into wedges

Directions

Step 1 Slice the steak into 1/2-inch thick slices over the grain.

Step 2 Whisk together soy sauce, sugar, cornstarch, and ginger in a bowl before sugar has dissolved and the mixture is smooth. Place the steak slices into the marinade, and stir until well-coated.

Step 3 Heat 1 tablespoon of vegetable oil in a wok or large skillet over medium-high heat, and place 1/3 of the steak strips into the hot oil. Cook and stir before beef is well-browned, around 3 minutes, and get rid of the beef from the wok to a bowl. Repeat twice more, with all of those other beef, and set the cooked beef aside.

Step 4 Return all the cooked beef to the hot wok, and stir in the onion. Toss the beef and onion together before onion begins to soften, about 2 minutes, then stir in the green pepper. Cook and stir the mixture before pepper has turned bright green and begun to become tender, about 2 minutes, then add the tomatoes, stir everything together, and serve.

Chinese Style Low Carb Meatballs

Ingredients

2 pounds ground pork
3 eaches large eggs
1/2 cup soy sauces, or to taste
1/2 cup thinly sliced green onions
3 cloves garlic, minced
1 teaspoon ground ginger

Directions

Step 1 Combine ground pork, eggs, soy sauce, green onions, garlic, and ginger in a big mixing bowl; using gloves, mix making use of your hands until all ingredients are incorporated well.

Step 2 Cover bowl with plastic wrap and chill in refrigerator 1 or 2 hours.

Step 3 Bring a saucepan of water to a boil.

Step 4 Employing a 1 teaspoon cookie scoop or a teaspoon, form pork mixture into small meatballs.

Step 5 Cook meatballs in small batches in boiling water until they float to the most effective and stay there for 3 minutes. Remove cooked meatballs from water with a slotted spoon.

Crispy Ginger Beef

Ingredients

3/4 cup cornstarch
1/2 cup water
2 large eggs eggs
1 pound flank steak, cut into thin strips
1/2 cup canola oils, or as needed
1 large carrot, cut into matchstick-size pieces
1 green bell pepper, cut into matchstick-size pieces
1 red bell pepper, cut into matchstick-size pieces
3 eaches green onions, chopped
1/4 cup minced fresh ginger root
5 eaches garlic cloves, minced
1/2 cup white sugar
1/4 cup rice vinegar
3 tablespoons soy sauce
1 tablespoon sesame oil
1 tablespoon red pepper flakes, or to taste

Directions

Step 1 Place cornstarch in a big bowl; gradually whisk in water until smooth. Whisk eggs into cornstarch mixture; toss steak strips in mixture to coat.

Step 2 Pour canola oil into wok 1-inch deep; heat oil over temperature until hot however, not smoking. Place 1/4 of the beef strips into hot oil; separate strips with a fork. Cook, stirring frequently, until coating is crisp and golden, around 3 minutes. Remove beef to drain on paper towels; repeat with remaining beef.

Step 3 Drain off all but 1 tablespoon oil; cook and stir carrot, green bell pepper, red bell pepper, green onions, ginger, and garlic over temperature until lightly browned however crisp, about 3 minutes.

Step 4 Whisk sugar, rice vinegar, soy sauce, sesame oil, and red pepper together in just a little bowl. Pour sauce mixture over vegetables in wok; bring mixture to a boil. Stir beef back again to vegetable mixture; cook and stir just until heated through, around 3 minutes.

Fried Spicy Noodles Singapore Style

Ingredients

3 bunches chinese mustard greens (gai choy), cut into 1-inch lengths
1 large onion, chopped
15 garlic clove (blank)s garlic cloves, chopped
10 peppers fresh red chili peppers, chopped
2/3 teaspoon ground fennel seed
2/3 teaspoon ground cumin seed
2/3 teaspoon ground coriander seed
2 teaspoons vegetable oil
1/2 pound boneless beef round steak, cut in thin slices
1/2 pound uncooked medium shrimp, peeled and deveined
1 tablespoon tomato paste
1 tablespoon black soy sauces (siew dam)
2 pounds fresh chinese yellow noodles
4 cups fresh bean sprouts
1 pinch salt to taste

Directions

Step 1 Separate the thin leafy components of the mustard greens from the thicker stems, and set them aside in separate bowls. Place the onion, garlic, chili peppers, fennel, cumin, and coriander in the duty bowl of a food processor, and pulse before mixture becomes a paste.

Step 2 Heat the oil in a wok or large skillet over medium-high heat, and cook and stir the onion-garlic mixture until it releases its fragrance, about 1 minute. Stir in the beef and shrimp, and cook and stir before beef is forget about pink and the shrimp are getting to be opaque, about 3 minutes.

Step 3 Stir in the tomato paste and soy sauce, and mix together until well combined. Stir in the noodles, tossing them with the sauce, beef, and shrimp until they have begun to soften, about 5 minutes. Add the mustard green stems, then cook and stir before stems have begun to soften and become translucent, about 3 more minutes.

Step 4 Stir the mustard green leafy parts into the dish, and the bean sprouts. Cook and stir everything together before mustard green leaves and bean sprouts are softened however bright in color, about 3 more minutes. Sprinkle with salt to taste.

Hong Kong-Style Chicken Chow Mein

Ingredients

14 ounces skinless, boneless chicken breasts, thinly sliced
1 egg white, beaten
2 teaspoons cornstarch
1 teaspoon sesame oil
1 (8-ounce) package chinese egg noodles
2 tablespoons vegetable oil, or as needed
1/2 cup chicken broth
3 eaches spring onions, chopped, or to taste
1 1/2 tablespoons light soy sauce
1 tablespoon rice wine (sake)
1/2 teaspoon ground white peppers
1/2 teaspoon ground black pepper
1 tablespoon cornstarch
2 teaspoons water
2 tablespoons oyster sauces
1 cup fresh bean sprouts, or to taste

Directions

Step 1 Mix chicken with egg white, 2 teaspoons cornstarch, and sesame oil in a bowl.

Step 2 Bring a big pot of water to a boil. Add egg noodles; cook until soft, about 4 minutes. Drain. Disseminate in some recoverable format towels to get rid of excess moisture.

Step 3 Heat vegetable oil in a wok over medium heat. Cook and stir noodles in the hot oil until golden brown, 3 to 5 minutes per side. Drain on paper towels.

Step 4 Stir chicken into the wok; cook, stirring frequently, until white, about 2 minutes. Transfer to a bowl employing a slotted spoon.

Step 5 Pour chicken stock into the wok; stir in spring onions, soy sauce, rice wine, white pepper, and black pepper.

Step 6 Mix 1 tablespoon cornstarch and water together in just a little bowl until smooth. Pour into the wok. Stir in oyster sauce. Add chicken and bean sprouts; cook and stir until chicken is tender and sauce is thickened, about 5 minutes. Serve over noodles.

Kung Pao Chicken

Ingredients

1 pound skinless, boneless chicken breasts halves - cut into chunks
2 tablespoons white wine
2 tablespoons soy sauce
2 tablespoons sesame oils, divided
2 tablespoons cornstarch, dissolved in
2 tablespoons water
1 ounce hot chile paste
1 teaspoon distilled white vinegar
2 teaspoons brown sugar
4 medium (4-1/8" long)s green onions, chopped
1 tablespoon chopped garlic
1 (8-ounce) can water chestnuts
4 ounces chopped peanuts

Directions

Step 1 TO CREATE Marinade: Combine 1 tablespoon wine, 1 tablespoon soy sauce, 1 tablespoon oil and 1 tablespoon cornstarch/water mixture and mix together. Place chicken pieces in a glass dish or bowl and add marinade. Toss to coat. Cover dish and place in refrigerator for about 30 minutes.

Step 2 TO CREATE Sauce: In just a little bowl combine 1 tablespoon wine, 1 tablespoon soy sauce, 1 tablespoon oil, 1 tablespoon cornstarch/water mixture, chili paste, vinegar and sugar. Mix together and add green onion, garlic, water chestnuts and peanuts. In a medium skillet, heat sauce slowly until aromatic.

Step 3 Meanwhile, remove chicken from marinade and saute in a big skillet until meat is white and juices run clear. When sauce is aromatic, add sauteed chicken to it and let simmer together until sauce thickens.

Mongolian Beef And Spring Onions

Ingredients

2 teaspoons vegetable oil

1 tablespoon finely chopped garlic

1/2 teaspoon grated fresh ginger root

1/2 cup soy sauce

1/2 cup water

2/3 cup dark brown sugar

1 pound beef flank steak, sliced 1/4 inch thick on the diagonal

1/4 cup cornstarch

1 cup vegetable oil for frying

2 bunches green onions, cut in 2-inch lengths

Directions

Step 1 Heat 2 teaspoons of vegetable oil in a saucepan over medium heat, and cook and stir the garlic and ginger until they release their fragrance, about 30 seconds. Pour in the soy sauce, water, and brown sugar. Enhance the heat to medium-high, and stir 4 minutes, before sugar has dissolved and the sauce boils and slightly thickens. Remove sauce from heat, and reserve.

Step 2 Place the sliced beef in to a bowl, and stir the cornstarch into the beef, coating it thoroughly. Let the beef and cornstarch to sit before most the juices from the meat have been absorbed by the cornstarch, about 10 minutes.

Step 3 Heat the vegetable oil in a deep-sided skillet or wok to 375 degrees F (190 degrees C).

Step 4 Shake excess cornstarch from the beef slices, and drop them into the hot oil, a few simultaneously. Stir briefly, and fry before edges become crisp and commence to brown, about 2 minutes. Get rid of the beef from the oil with a big slotted spoon, and invite to drain in a few recoverable format towels to remove excess oil.

Step 5 Pour the oil from the skillet or wok, and return the pan to medium heat. Return the beef slices to the pan, stir briefly, and pour in the reserved sauce. Stir several times to combine, and add the green onions. Bring the mixture to a boil, and cook before onions have softened and turned bright green, about 2 minutes.

Pad Thai Quinoa Bowl

Ingredients

4 cups low-sodium chicken broth
2 cups quinoa, rinsed and drained
1 tablespoon coconut oils, divided
1 large boneless, skinless chicken breast, cut into thin strips
3/4 cup shredded cabbage
1/2 cup edamame
1/4 cup diced broccoli stems
2 carrot, (7-1/2")s carrots, cut into matchsticks
2 eaches green onions, chopped
3 large eggs eggs
1 teaspoon sesame oil
1/4 cup natural peanut butter
1/4 cup reduced-sodium soy sauce
3 tablespoons rice vinegar
2 tablespoons chili garlic sauce
2 tablespoons chopped fresh ginger
3 cloves garlic, minced
1 teaspoon sesame oil
1/2 cup salted peanuts, chopped
3 tablespoons chopped fresh cilantro

Directions

Step 1 Bring chicken broth and quinoa to a boil in a saucepan. Reduce heat to medium-low, cover, and simmer until quinoa is tender, 15 to 20 minutes. Reserve.

Step 2 Heat 1 1/2 teaspoons coconut oil in a wok or large skillet over medium-high heat. Add chicken; stir until cooked through; about 5 minutes. Remove chicken from wok. Heat remaining 1 1/2 teaspoons coconut oil. Add cabbage, edamame, broccoli, carrot, and green onions and saute until vegetables soften slightly, 2-3 minutes.

Step 3 Whisk eggs with sesame oil in just a little bowl. Push vegetables to the sides of the wok to make a well in the guts; pour eggs in and stir to scramble, around 3 minutes.

Step 4 Combine peanut butter, soy sauce, rice vinegar, chili garlic sauce, ginger, garlic, and sesame oil together in just a little bowl. Pour Thai peanut sauce over vegetable and egg mixture in the wok.

Step 5 Return chicken to the wok and add quinoa; mix well to combine. Stir in chopped peanuts and cilantro and serve.

Pork And Shrimp Pancit

Ingredients

1 (6.75 ounce) package rice noodle
5 tablespoons vegetable oil, divided
1 small onion, minced
2 cloves garlic, minced
1/2 teaspoon ground ginger
1 1/2 cups cooked small shrimp, diced
1 1/2 cups chopped cooked pork
4 cups shredded bok choy
3 tablespoons oyster sauces
1/4 cup chicken broth
1/4 teaspoon crushed red pepper flakes
1 green onion, minced

Directions

Step 1 Soak the rice noodles in warm water for 20 minutes; drain.

Step 2 Heat 3 tablespoons oil in a wok or large heavy skillet over medium-high heat. Saute noodles for 1 minute. Transfer to serving dish, and keep warm. Add remaining 2 tablespoons oil to skillet, and saute onion, garlic, ginger, shrimp and pork for 1 minute.

Step 3 Stir in bok choy, oyster sauce and chicken broth. Season with pepper flakes. Cover, and cook for 1 minute, or until bok choy is wilted. Spoon over noodles, and garnish with minced green onion.

Shrimp With Broccoli In Garlic Sauce

Ingredients

2 cups fresh broccoli florets
1 tablespoon water
2 tablespoons peanut oil
4 large cloves garlic, minced
1 cup low-sodium chicken broth
1 tablespoon soy sauce
1 tablespoon oyster sauces
2 teaspoons grated fresh ginger root
1 pound uncooked medium shrimp, peeled and deveined
1/4 cup canned water chestnuts, drained
2 tablespoons cornstarch

Directions

Step 1 Combine broccoli and water in a glass bowl; steam in microwave oven until slightly tender, 2-3 minutes.

Step 2 Heat peanut oil in a big skillet or wok over medium-high heat. Cook garlic in hot oil until fragrant, about 1 minute. Reduce heat to low; add chicken broth, soy sauce, oyster sauce, and ginger root to the garlic. Bring the mixture to a boil and add the shrimp; cook and stir before shrimp turn pink, 3 to 4 minutes.

Toss steamed broccoli and water chestnuts with the shrimp mixture to coat with the sauce. Stir cornstarch into the mixture 1 tablespoon simultaneously before sauce thickens, about 5 minutes.

April's Chicken Fried Rice

Ingredients

2 cups uncooked white rice
1 tablespoon butter
2 whole breast (blank)s skinless, boneless chicken breasts halves - cubed
salt to taste
2 large eggs eggs, beaten
3/4 cup sliced mushrooms
2 medium (4-1/8" long)s green onions, chopped
1 tablespoon soy sauces, or to taste

Directions

Step 1 In a saucepan bring 4 cups water to a boil. Add rice and stir. Reduce heat, cover and simmer for 20 minutes.

Step 2 Heat butter in a big skillet over medium-high heat. Brown chicken in butter and season with salt to taste. Set chicken aside.

Step 3 Transfer cooked rice to the skillet where in fact the chicken was cooked, stirring to brown.

Step 4 In another skillet, scramble eggs.

Step 5 To the rice add chicken, mushrooms, green onions, eggs and soy sauce to taste.

Asian Fire Meat

Ingredients

1/2 cup soy sauce
1 tablespoon sesame oil
2 tablespoons brown sugar
3 cloves garlic, crushed
1 large red onion, chopped
ground black pepper to taste
1 teaspoon red pepper flakes
2 tablespoons sesame seeds
2 leeks leeks, chopped
1 small carrot, chopped
1 pound beef round steak, sliced paper thin

Directions

Step 1 In a big bowl, mix together the soy sauce, sesame oil, brown sugar, garlic, and red onion. Stir in the black pepper, red pepper flakes, sesame seeds, leeks and carrot. Mix in the meat you to ultimately make certain even coating. Cover and let marinate for at least 2 hours or overnight.

Step 2 Brush underneath half of a wok with cooking oil, and heat over medium-high heat. Devote all of the meat and marinade simultaneously, and cook stirring constantly. The meat will be cooked after just a few minutes. Remove from heat and serve with rice or noodles. For Korean-style fire meat, roll the meat mixture up in a leaf of red lettuce.

Basic Chinese Stir Fry Vegetables

Ingredients

2 cups uncooked brown rice
4 cups water
1 tablespoon safflower oil
1/3 cup leeks, chopped
2 cloves garlic
1 teaspoon minced fresh ginger root
1 cup zucchini, chopped
1 cup carrots, chopped
1 cup yellow squash, chopped
1 pinch sea salt to taste

Directions

Step 1 Bring the brown rice and water to a boil in a saucepan over temperature. Reduce the heat to medium-low, cover, and simmer before rice is tender, and the liquid has been absorbed, 45 to 50 minutes.

Step 2 Heat the safflower oil in a skillet over medium heat. Stir in the leeks, garlic, and ginger; cook and stir before leeks have softened, about 5 minutes. Stir in the zucchini, carrots, and yellow squash. Season with salt. Continue cooking and stirring before vegetables have softened, about 2 minutes. Serve over brown rice.

Beef And Cabbage Stir Fry

Ingredients

2 tablespoons vegetable oil
4 cloves garlic, chopped
1/2 pound ground beef
1/2 small head cabbage, shredded
1 red bell pepper, cut into strips
2 tablespoons soy sauce
1 teaspoon cornstarch
1/2 cup cold water
1 teaspoon ground black pepper, or
to taste
1 pinch salt, to taste

Directions

Step 1 Heat a wok or large skillet over medium-high heat, and add oil. Saute garlic for about 5 seconds, then add ground beef. Stir-fry until beef is evenly brown, 5 to 7 minutes; drain body fat.

Step 2 Stir in cabbage and pepper, and cook until vegetables are tender and beef is fully cooked. Stir in soy sauce. Mix together cornstarch and water, and stir in. Season with pepper; add salt to taste. Cook, stirring, until sauce has thickened.

Bitter Melon And Black Bean Sauce Beef

Ingredients

1 ice cubes
1 bitter melon, seeded and sliced
2 teaspoons soy sauces, divided
2 teaspoons cornstarch, divided
1/4 teaspoon baking soda
6 ounces beef, sliced
1 tablespoon oils
1 teaspoon oils
1/2 onion, sliced
2 cloves garlic
1 tablespoon chopped fresh ginger
1 tablespoon black bean sauces
1 tablespoon oyster sauces
1 pinch white sugar, or to taste
3/4 cup water
1 teaspoon water
1 pinch salt to taste

Directions

Step 1 Fill a bowl with ice; add enough salted water to create an ice bath. Bring a big pot of lightly salted water to a boil. Cook the bitter melon in the boiling water until tender yet firm, about 2 minutes; strain the melon. Place the melon into the ice bath; allow to sit until bitterness is extracted, about 1 hour. Drain melon.

Step 2 Whisk 1 teaspoon soy sauce, 1 teaspoon cornstarch, and baking soda together in a bowl. Add beef and toss to evenly coat. Marinate in the refrigerator for just 1 hour.

Step 3 Heat wok, or a big skillet, on high until smoking. Add 1 tablespoon oil. Lay beef evenly over underneath of the wok; cook until browned, about 2 minutes per side. Remove beef. Pour in 1 teaspoon of oil; allow to heat. Add onion, garlic, and ginger; cook and stir until fragrant, about 30 seconds. Stir in bitter melon; cook until combined, about 1 minute.

Step 4 Stir black bean sauce into melon mixture. Stir in remaining soy sauce, oyster sauce, and sugar. Pour in 3/4 cup water; cover and let simmer until flavors combine, 2-3 minutes. Uncover and mix in remaining cornstarch and 1 teaspoon water and stir until thickened.

Broccoli And Carrot Stir Fry

Ingredients

5 1/2 cups broccoli florets
1 carrot, thinly sliced
2 teaspoons water
1 teaspoon cornstarch
1 teaspoon chicken bouillon granules,
or to taste
1 pinch salt to taste
2 tablespoons peanut oil

Directions

Step 1 Bring a big pot of lightly salted water to a boil. Add broccoli and cook uncovered until bright green, about 2 minutes. Transfer broccoli to a bowl of ice water employing a slotted spoon and immerse for some minutes in order to avoid the cooking process. Drain.

Step 2 Bring water back to a boil in the same large pot; add sliced carrot and cook for 1 minute. Drain.

Step 3 Mix water and cornstarch together in a bowl until smooth. Add chicken granules and salt and mix well.

Step 4 Heat peanut oil in a wok or large skillet over temperature; saute broccoli and carrots for 2 minutes. Add cornstarch mixture; cook and stir until vegetables are coated evenly, 1 or 2 minutes.

Chicken And Multi-Grain Stir Fry

Ingredients

1 bag minute® multi-grain medley, uncooked
1 cup chicken broth
2 large eggs, lightly beaten
1/2 teaspoon sesame oil
2 tablespoons olive oils, divided
2 cloves garlic, chopped
1/2 cup red onions, thinly sliced
1/2 cup snap peas
1/2 cup broccoli florets
1/2 cup red bell pepper, sliced
1/2 teaspoon chinese five-spice powder
2 cups cooked chicken, shredded

Directions

Step 1 Prepare Multi-Grain Medley according to package directions, substituting broth for water. In just a little bowl, whisk together eggs and sesame oil.

Step 2 In a big skillet, heat 1/2 tablespoon coconut oil over medium-low heat.

Step 3 Quickly soft scramble eggs. Remove from skillet and keep warm. Heat remaining coconut oil over medium heat. Add garlic, onions, peas, broccoli, bell peppers and five spice powder and sauté for 3 minutes. Step 4 Add chicken, Multi-Grain Medley and eggs; sauté 2 more minutes or until vegetables are crisp-tender.

Chicken And Snow Peas

Ingredients

1 cup chicken broth
3 tablespoons soy sauce
1 tablespoon cornstarch
1 tablespoon ground ginger
2 tablespoons vegetable oil
4 large skinless, boneless chicken breasts halves, cubed
2 cloves garlic, minced
1 1/2 cups sliced fresh mushrooms
2 (8-ounce) cans sliced water chestnuts, drained
3 cups snow peas
1 tablespoon sesame seeds

Directions

Step 1 Whisk the chicken broth, soy sauce, cornstarch, and ginger together in just a little bowl; reserve.

Step 2 Heat oil in a big skillet or wok. Cook and stir chicken and garlic in the oil until chicken is cooked through, 8 to 10 minutes. Stir in mushrooms, water chestnuts, and reserved chicken broth mixture. Cook until sauce begins to thicken, 3 to 5 minutes.

Step 3 Stir snow peas into the pan and cook until tender, 3 to 5 minutes. Transfer to a platter and sprinkle with sesame seeds before serving.

Chicken Broccoli Ca - Unieng's Style

Ingredients

12 ounces boneless skinless chicken breast halves boneless skinless chicken breast halves cut into bite-sized pieces
1 tablespoon oysters oyster sauce
2 tablespoons soy sauce dark soy sauce
3 tablespoons vegetable oil vegetable oil
2 cloves garlic garlic chopped
1 onion large onion cut into rings
1/2 cup water water
1 teaspoon black pepper ground black pepper
1 teaspoon sugar white sugar
1/2 head bok choy medium bok choy chopped
1 head broccoli small broccoli chopped
1 tablespoon cornstarch cornstarch mixed with equal parts water

Directions
Step 1 In a big bowl, combine chicken, oyster sauce and soy sauce. Reserve for a quarter-hour.
Step 2 Heat oil in a wok or large heavy skillet over medium heat. Saute garlic and onion until soft and translucent. Increase heat to high. Add chicken and marinade, then stir-fry until light golden brown, about

10 minutes. Stir in water, pepper and sugar. Add bok choy and broccoli, and cook stirring until soft, about 10 minutes. Pour in the cornstarch mixture, and cook until sauce is thickened, about 5 minutes.

Chicken Yakisoba

Ingredients

2 tablespoons canola oil
1 tablespoon sesame oil
2 eaches skinless, boneless chicken breasts halves - cut into bite-size pieces
2 cloves garlic, minced
2 tablespoons asian-style chile paste
1/2 cup soy sauce
1 tablespoon canola oil
1/2 medium head cabbage, thinly sliced
1 onion, sliced
2 carrot, (7-1/2")s carrots, cut into matchsticks
1 tablespoon salt
2 pounds cooked yakisoba noodles
2 tablespoons pickled ginger, or to taste

Directions

Step 1 Heat 2 tablespoons canola oil and sesame oil in a big skillet over medium-high heat. Cook and stir chicken and garlic in hot oil until fragrant, about 1 minute. Stir chile paste into chicken mixture; cook and stir until chicken is completely browned, 3 to 4 minutes. Add soy sauce and simmer for 2 minutes. Pour chicken and sauce in to a bowl.

Step 2 Heat 1 tablespoon canola oil in the skillet over medium-high heat; cook and stir cabbage, onion, carrots, and salt in hot oil until cabbage is wilted, 3 to 4 minutes.

Step 3 Stir the chicken mixture into the cabbage mixture. Add noodles; cook and stir until noodles are hot and chicken is forget about pink inside, 3 to 4 minutes. Garnish with pickled ginger.

Chinese New Year Sweet Rice

Ingredients

3 cups uncooked jasmine rice
1 1/2 cups water
2 cups dried shiitake mushrooms
3 tablespoons oyster sauces, divided
2 tablespoons soy sauce
2 tablespoons cornstarch
1 teaspoon salt
1 tablespoon white sugar
1 tablespoon red wine
3 links lop chong (chinese-style sausage)
1 tablespoon sesame oil
1 pound fresh shrimp - peeled, deveined, and diced
1/4 pound cooked pork link sausages, diced
1 bunch green onions, diced
1 cup fresh water chestnuts, peeled and diced
1 1/2 cups frozen green peas

Directions
Step 1 Place the jasmine rice and water in a medium saucepan. Cover and let stand at least 1 hour, before

water has been absorbed. Transfer to a steamer basket and fluff with a fork. Steam 20 minutes, or until tender.

Step 2 Place the dried mushrooms in a bowl with enough tepid to warm water to cover. Soak 30 mins or until tender. Drain, remove stems, and slice.

Step 3 In just a little bowl, mix 1 tablespoon oyster sauce, soy sauce, cornstarch, salt, sugar, and burgandy or merlot wine. Place mushrooms in the bowl, and marinate at least quarter-hour.

Step 4 In the steamer basket, steam the mushrooms and Chinese-style sausage 15 to 20 minutes. Remove from heat and chop.

Step 5 Heat the sesame oil in a big wok over temperature. Toss in the shrimp and cook one or two 2 minutes, until nearly opaque. Stir in the mushrooms, Chinese-style sausage, pork sausage, green onion, and water chestnuts. Cook and stir about 2 minutes. Mix in the rice and remaining oyster sauce. Cook another 3 to 4 minutes. Remove from heat and toss in the peas. Serve when the peas are heated through.

Chinese Noodle Chicken

Ingredients

4 breast half, bone and skin removed
(blank)s skinless, boneless chicken
breasts
1 tablespoon vegetable oil
1/2 cup sliced onions
2 cups broccoli florets
2 medium (blank)s carrots, julienned
2 cups snow peas
4 cups dry chinese noodles
1/4 cup teriyaki sauce

Directions

Step 1 In a big skillet brown chicken in oil, stirring constantly until juices run clear.

Step 2 Add the onion, broccoli, carrots and peas. Cover skillet and steam for 2 minutes.

Step 3 Add the Chinese noodles and teriyaki sauce. Stir noodles into chicken/vegetable mixture, making sure they are coated with sauce. When the noodles wilt, serve.

Chinese Stir-Fried Sticky Rice With Chinese Sausage

Ingredients

2 cups glutinous rice
8 eaches dried shiitake mushrooms
1/3 cup dried shrimp
2 eaches dried scallops
1 teaspoon olive oil
3 large eggs eggs, beaten
3 links chinese sausages, diced
2 cups hot water, or more as needed
2 tablespoons light soy sauces, or to taste
2 teaspoons dark soy sauce
1 teaspoon white sugar
1/2 cup chopped cilantro, or to taste

Directions

Step 1 Soak rice in a big bowl of water until mostly translucent, about 4 hours. Rinse and drain thoroughly.
Step 2 Soak mushrooms, shrimp, and scallops in 3 separate bowls of water until softened, about quarter-hour. Drain, reserving mushroom water and discarding other water. Chop mushrooms, shrimp, and scallops into small pieces.
Step 3 Heat coconut oil in a big skillet over medium heat. Pour eggs into skillet, swirling to disseminate in to

a thin layer. Cook until mostly firm, about 1 minute. Flip and cook until forget about runny, 3 to 5 minutes.

Step 4 Transfer egg to a cutting board and invite to cool slightly. Roll in to a long tube and slice into thin ribbons.

Step 5 Stir Chinese sausage into the same skillet over medium heat. Cook and stir until fragrant and several of the oil is released, around 3 minutes. Add mushrooms, shrimp, and scallops; cook for 3 to 5 minutes. Transfer sausage mixture to a bowl.

Step 6 Stir drained rice into the skillet. Cook and stir until lightly toasted, one or two 2 minutes. Pour in reserved mushroom water, stirring constantly until water is absorbed. Add tepid to warm water, 1/2 cup simultaneously, stirring until water is absorbed between each addition. Cook until rice is softened, about 25 minutes.

Step 7 Season rice with light soy sauce, dark soy sauce, and sugar. Stir in egg ribbons and sausage mixture. Top with cilantro before serving.

Chinese Style Ground Pork And Tofu

Ingredients

2 cloves garlic, minced
2 tablespoons olive oil
1 pound ground pork
1 (14-ounce) package firm tofu, cubed
1 tablespoon spicy black bean sauces
2 teaspoons soy sauces to taste
2 tablespoons dry sherry
1 bunch green onions, chopped

Directions

Step 1 Cook garlic in the fundamental essential olive oil over medium-high heat in a big saucepan until lightly browned and fragrant. Add underneath pork and brown, stirring frequently to break it up. Stir in the tofu, reduce the heat to medium, and cook to reheat, stirring occasionally, around 3 minutes. Season with black bean sauce, soy sauce, sherry, and green onions.

Chinese Take-Out Shrimp With Garlic

Ingredients

2 tablespoons canola oil
10 cloves garlic, chopped
1 teaspoon minced fresh ginger root
1 (8-ounce) can sliced water chestnuts, drained
1 cup snow peas
1 cup small white button mushrooms
1 teaspoon crushed red pepper flakes
1/2 teaspoon salt
1 teaspoon ground black pepper
1 pound peeled and deveined jumbo shrimp
1/2 cup chicken broth
1 tablespoon rice vinegar
2 tablespoons fish sauces
2 tablespoons dry sherry
1 tablespoon cornstarch
1 tablespoon water

Directions

Step 1 Heat oil in wok or large skillet until scorching. Cook and stir garlic and ginger in the hot oil until fragrant, about 30 seconds. Add the water chestnuts, snow peas, mushrooms, red pepper flakes, salt, pepper, and shrimp to the pan. Cook, stirring, until shrimp turns pink, 2-3 minutes.

Step 2 Combine the chicken broth, rice vinegar, fish sauce, and dry sherry in just a little bowl. Pour into the shrimp mixture; cook and stir briefly to combine. Combine the cornstarch and water and stir into the wok. Stir until sauce has thickened, about 2 minutes.

Citrus Carp

Ingredients

1/2 peel of small mandarin orange
3 pounds whole carp, cleaned and scaled
2 teaspoons salt
1/4 cup cornstarch
2 cups sesame oil
2 1/2 tablespoons chopped garlic
3 tablespoons minced fresh ginger root
1/4 cup chopped green onions
3 tablespoons dry sherry
1 tablespoon black bean sauces
2 tablespoons soy sauce
1 tablespoon white sugar
6 tablespoons chicken stock

Directions

Step 1 Soak the orange peel in warm water for 20 minutes or until it truly is soft. Drain, and rinse the peel under running water. Squeeze out extra liquid. Chop the peel and reserve.

Step 2 Make 3 or 4 slashes on either side of the fish and rub the fish with salt. Sprinkle the fish on both sides with cornstarch.

Third Step 3 Heat oil in a frying pan or wok. When the oil is hot, deep fry the fish on both sides for approximately 4-6 minutes per side; both sides of the fish should be browned. Get rid of the fish from the pan and invite it drain in some recoverable format towels

Step 4 Dispense of all but 2 tablespoons of the oil (leave that oil in the pan or wok). Bring the oil back to an increased heat, mix in the orange peel, garlic, ginger, and green onions. Stir fry for 30 seconds. Add sherry, bean sauce, soy sauce, sugar and chicken stock. Mix well, then add the fish to the mixture. Cover and let cook for 8 minutes. Serve immediately.

Comida China

Ingredients

1 skinless, boneless chicken breast half, cut into bite-size pieces
1 pinch salt and ground black pepper to taste
2 tablespoons all-purpose flour
2 tablespoons olive oils, or as needed, divided
1 clove garlic, minced
1 cup cauliflower florets
1 cup broccoli florets
1/2 small onion, chopped
1 zucchini, chopped
1 carrot, chopped
1 celery rib, chopped
2 tablespoons soy sauce
2 tablespoons oyster sauces

Directions

Step 1 Season chicken with salt and pepper. Place flour in a shallow bowl. Gently press chicken into the flour to coat and eliminate the excess flour.

Step 2 Heat 1 tablespoon coconut oil in a skillet over medium-high heat; saute chicken until browned on all sides, about 5 minutes. Remove skillet from heat.

Step 3 Heat remaining coconut oil in a wok or large skillet over medium heat; cook and stir garlic until fragrant, about 30 seconds. Add cauliflower, broccoli, onion, zucchini, carrot, and celery; cook and stir until vegetables are slightly tender, 3 to 4 minutes. Add chicken, soy sauce, and oyster sauce to vegetable mixture; cook and stir until chicken is forget about pink in the guts and vegetables reach desired tenderness, about 5 minutes.

Crab Fried Rice

Ingredients

2/3 cup white rice uncooked long grain white rice

1 <small>1/3</small> cups water water

3 tablespoons vegetable oil vegetable oil

2 onions medium onions cut into wedges

3 cloves garlic garlic chopped

1/2 tablespoon sugar white sugar

2 teaspoons salt salt

1 egg egg beaten

1/4 pound crabmeat cooked crabmeat

3 green onions medium (4-1/8" long)s green onions chopped

1 tablespoon cilantro chopped cilantro

1/2 cucumber cucumber sliced

1 lime lime sliced

Directions

Step 1 Place the rice and water in a saucepan, and bring to a boil. Reduce heat, cover, and simmer for 20 minutes.

Step 2 Heat the oil in a wok over medium heat. Cook and stir the onions and garlic in the hot oil until tender.

Mix in the rice, sugar, and salt, and cook 5 minutes, until well blended. Stir in the egg before rice is coated. Increase heat to high, and mix in the crabmeat, green onions, and cilantro. Continue cooking 2 to 5 minutes, before crab is heated through. Garnish with the cucumber and lime slices to serve.

Duck Fried Rice

Ingredients

1 cup chopped chinese roast duck meat, skin and fat separated and set aside
1/2 cup thinly sliced chinese barbecued pork
6 medium (4-1/8" long)s green onions, thinly sliced
2 tablespoons soy sauce
2 large eggs eggs, beaten
3 cups cooked long-grain rice
1 pinch salt and pepper to taste

Directions

Step 1 Cook the duck skin and fat in a wok or large skillet over medium heat before skin is crispy, and the fat has rendered, about 10 minutes. Increase heat to medium-high, and stir in the duck meat, pork, half of the green onions, and the soy sauce. Cook and stir before meats are heated through, about 5 minutes.

Step 2 Add rice and toss together until rice is hot and sizzling, about 5 minutes. Make a wide well in the heart of the rice, exposing underneath of the pan. Pour in the beaten eggs and stir before eggs have scrambled. Then stir the scrambled eggs into the rice combined with the remaining green onions. Toss and stir before rice is fairly hot, about 5 minutes. Season to taste with salt and pepper before serving.

Flavorful Beef Stir-Fry

Ingredients

2 cups brown rice
4 cups water
2 tablespoons cornstarch
2 teaspoons white sugar
6 tablespoons soy sauce
1/4 cup white wine
1 tablespoon minced fresh ginger
1 pound boneless beef round steak, cut into thin strips
1 tablespoon vegetable oil
3 cups broccoli florets
2 medium (blank)s carrots, thinly sliced
1 (6-ounce) package frozen pea pods, thawed
2 tablespoons chopped onions
1 (8-ounce) can sliced water chestnuts, undrained
1 cup chinese cabbage
2 large heads bok choy, chopped
1 tablespoon vegetable oil

Directions
Step 1 Bring brown rice and water to a boil in a saucepan over temperature. Reduce heat to medium-

low, cover, and simmer until rice is tender, and liquid has been absorbed, 45 to 50 minutes.

Step 2 Combine cornstarch, sugar, soy sauce, and wine in just a little bowl until smooth. Stir in ginger; toss beef in sauce to coat.

Step 3 Heat 1 tablespoon oil in a big skillet over medium-high heat. Cook and stir broccoli, carrots, pea pods, and onion for 1 minute. Stir in water chestnuts, Chinese cabbage, and bok choy; cover and simmer until vegetables are tender, about 4 minutes. Remove from skillet and keep warm.

Step 4 In same skillet, heat 1 tablespoon oil over medium-high heat. Cook and stir beef until desired amount of doneness, about 2 minutes per side for medium. Return vegetables to skillet; cook and stir until heated through, around 3 minutes. Serve over rice.

Ginger Chicken With Cashews

Ingredients

1 1/2 cups chicken broth
1/2 cup soy sauce
1 tablespoon cornstarch
3/4 teaspoon ground ginger
3/4 teaspoon brown sugar
1/4 cup cornstarch
1 1/2 teaspoons ground ginger
1/4 teaspoon curry powder
2 pounds skinless, boneless chicken breasts meat - cut into cubes
3 tablespoons extra-virgin olive oil
1 tablespoon sesame oil
3 eaches green onions, chopped
1 bell pepper, chopped
1 teaspoon sesame seeds
1/2 cup cashews

Directions

Step 1 Whisk together the chicken broth, soy sauce, 1 tablespoon cornstarch, 3/4 teaspoon ground ginger, and brown sugar in a bowl.

Step 2 Combine 1/4 cup cornstarch, 1 1/2 teaspoons ground ginger, and curry powder in a big, sealable plastic bag and shake to mix. Add the chicken to the bag and toss until well coated.

Step 3 Heat the fundamental essential olive oil and sesame oil in a wok or large skillet over temperature. Cook and stir the chicken in the hot oil until golden brown, 3 to 5 minutes. Add the green onions and bell pepper to the pan, cooking another 2-3 minutes. Stir the sauce mixture into the chicken and vegetable mixture; reduce heat to medium. Sprinkle sesame seeds over the dish and bring to a boil; allow to boil before sauce thickens, 3 to 5 minutes. Remove from heat; add cashews and toss to serve.

Ginger Veggie Stir-Fry

Ingredients

1 tablespoon cornstarch
1 1/2 cloves garlic, crushed
2 teaspoons chopped fresh ginger root, divided
1/4 cup vegetable oil, divided
1 small head broccoli, cut into florets
1/2 cup snow peas
3/4 cup julienned carrots
1/2 cup halved green beans
2 tablespoons soy sauce
2 1/2 tablespoons water
1/4 cup chopped onions
1/2 tablespoon salt

Directions

Step 1 In a big bowl, blend cornstarch, garlic, 1 teaspoon ginger, and 2 tablespoons vegetable oil until cornstarch is dissolved. Mix in broccoli, snow peas, carrots, and green beans, tossing to lightly coat.

Step 2 Heat remaining 2 tablespoons oil in a big skillet or wok over medium heat. Cook vegetables in oil for 2 minutes, stirring constantly in order to avoid burning. Stir in soy sauce and water. Mix in onion, salt, and remaining 1 teaspoon ginger. Cook until vegetables are tender however crisp.

Hoisin Pork Stir Fry

Ingredients

1 pound boneless pork chops, cut into stir-fry strips
1 tablespoon hoisin sauce
1 tablespoon cornstarch
2 tablespoons hoisin sauce
1/4 cup chicken broth
1 tablespoon cornstarch
1 tablespoon rice vinegar
1 tablespoon white sugar
1 teaspoon red pepper flakes, or to taste
1 tablespoon sesame oil
2 cloves garlic, minced
2 teaspoons minced fresh ginger root
1 carrot, peeled and sliced
1 green bell pepper, sliced
1 (4-ounce) can sliced water chestnuts, drained
2 stalks (blank)s green onions, sliced

Directions
Step 1 Mix the sliced pork, 1 tablespoon hoisin sauce, and 1 tablespoon cornstarch together in a bowl. Reserve. Combine all of those other 2 tablespoons

hoisin sauce, chicken broth, and 1 tablespoon cornstarch with rice vinegar, sugar, and cayenne pepper in normal size bowl. Reserve.

Step 2 Heat the sesame oil in a skillet over medium-high heat. Stir in the pork; cook and stir before pork begins to brown, about 5 minutes. Add the garlic and ginger; cook and stir until fragrant. Mix in the carrot, bell pepper, and water chestnuts, cooking before carrots are tender. Stir in the reserved hoisin sauce mixture and continue cooking and stirring before flavors are combined, around 3 minutes.

Hong Kong Sweet And Sour Pork

Ingredients

2 teaspoons light soy sauce
teaspoon ? white sugar
2 teaspoons potatoes starch
1 teaspoon sesame oil
1 pinch ground black pepper to taste
1 pound pork loin, cut into 1-inch cubes
1 cup water
2 tablespoons white vinegar
1/4 cup ketchup
1/4 cup white sugar
1 pinch salt
2 teaspoons potatoes starch
1 dash red food coloring
1 egg, beaten
1 cup potatoes starch
2 cups peanut oil for frying
1 green bell pepper, cut into large chunks
2 eaches cayenne peppers, sliced
4 rings slices canned pineapple, chopped
2 cloves garlic, sliced
2 eaches green onions, sliced

Directions

Step 1 Whisk together the soy sauce, sugar, 2 teaspoons potato starch, sesame oil, and black pepper in a big bowl. Mix the pork into the marinade and turn until all the pork is covered. Allow to rest for quarter-hour.

Step 2 To make the sauce, whisk together the water, vinegar, ketchup, 1/4 cup sugar, salt, 2 teaspoons potato starch, and red food coloring in another bowl. Reserve.

Third Step 3 Dip the pork pieces in the beaten egg, then dredge in the 1 cup potato starch. Use your hand to press the starch onto the pork, assuring a consistent coating.

Step 4 Heat the peanut oil in a wok over medium-high heat to a temperature of 375 degrees F (190 degrees C).

Step 5 Fry the pork pieces in the hot oil until crisp and light brown, 4 to 5 minutes. Get rid of the pork from the oil and drain, keeping the oil hot. Return the drained pork pieces to the hot oil for 30 seconds more. Remove and drain again. Pour off all but 1 tablespoon of oil from the wok.

Step 6 Heat 1 tablespoon of reserved oil in the wok over medium heat. Cook the green bell pepper, cayenne pepper, pineapple, garlic, and green onion in the heated oil for about 5 minutes. Add the sauce and stir until it thickens. Stir in the pork and toss before pork is coated with sauce. Remove from heat and serve.

Hunan Peppered Pork

Ingredients

3 tablespoons vegetable oil, or more as needed, divided
2 cloves garlic, crushed
1 ounce fresh ginger, minced
1 pound pork tenderloin, sliced into thin strips, or to taste
3 eaches hot long green chile peppers, sliced into thin strips, or more to taste
1 pinch salt to taste
2 teaspoons soy sauces, or to taste

Directions

Step 1 Heat 1 tablespoon oil in a wok or large skillet over medium-high heat until smoking; saute garlic and ginger until fragrant, 30 seconds to at least one 1 minute. Add pork to wok; cook and stir until cooked through, 5 to 7 minutes. Transfer pork to a plate.

Step 2 Pour remaining 2 tablespoons oil into the same wok over medium-high heat; saute chile peppers until well-coated with oil and fragrant, about 2 minutes. Add pork to chile peppers and generously season with salt. Cook and stir mixture until peppers are tender, 5 to 7 minutes more. Mix enough soy sauce into pork mixture to add color and taste for desired saltiness.

Ken Shoe Green Beans

Ingredients

1/2 cup peanut oil for frying
1 pound fresh green beans, trimmed
and cut into 2-inch pieces
1 tablespoon minced fresh ginger root
1 tablespoon minced garlic
1 1/2 teaspoons dark soy sauce
1/2 teaspoon white sugar
1 pinch black pepper

Directions

Step 1 Heat the peanut oil in a wok or skillet with high sides over medium-high heat until almost smoking; add the green beans. Quickly cook and stir the beans in the hot oil until they are bright green and must show brown spots, about 2 minutes. Get rid of the beans to a bowl. Drain all but 2 tablespoons of oil from the pan and get back to heat. Cook and stir the ginger and garlic in the oil until they have started to brown, about 2 minutes. Return the green beans to the wok; add the dark soy sauce, sugar, and black pepper. Cook until hot; about 30 more seconds.

Kung Pao Chicken Stir-Fry

Ingredients

1 1/2 pounds skinless, boneless chicken breasts halves, cut into cubes
1 tablespoon cornstarch
1 pinch salt and pepper to taste
1 pinch chinese five-spice powder, or to taste
3/4 cup water
2 tablespoons soy sauce
2 tablespoons brown sugar
1 tablespoon asian (toasted) sesame oil
1 tablespoon cornstarch
1 1/2 teaspoons rice vinegar
1 pinch chinese five-spice powder
2 tablespoons vegetable oil, divided
1 onion, diced
1 stalk celery, diced
4 cloves garlic, chopped
1 teaspoon red pepper flakes, or to taste
1/3 cup roasted peanuts, or to taste

Directions

Step 1 Mix the chicken, 1 tablespoon of cornstarch, salt, pepper, and 1 pinch of five-spice powder together in a bowl before chicken is coated, and reserve.

Step 2 Whisk together water, soy sauce, brown sugar, sesame oil, 1 tablespoon of cornstarch, rice vinegar, and 1 pinch of five-spice powder in a bowl before mixture is smooth, and reserve.

Step 3 Place 1 tablespoon of oil in a wok or large skillet over medium-high heat, and cook and stir the chicken mixture before chicken is browned, about 5 minutes. Get rid of the chicken from the wok, and reserve.

Step 4 Pour 1 more tablespoon of oil into the heated wok, and stir in the onion, celery, garlic, and red pepper flakes. Cook and stir the vegetables until linked with emotions . become tender, around 3 minutes. Pour in the cornstarch mixture, and cook and stir before sauce thickens, about 1 minute. Get rid of the wok from heat, lightly stir in the cooked chicken and peanuts, and serve.

Mabo Dofu Recipe

Ingredients

1 tablespoon sesame oil
1 (1/2 inch) piece fresh ginger, minced
1 clove garlic, minced, or more to taste
1/2 pound ground pork
2 teaspoons chili bean sauces (toban djan)
1 tablespoon soy sauce
2 tablespoons sake
2 teaspoons oyster sauces
1 (12-ounce) package tofu, cut into 1/2-inch squares
1/2 cup water, or more if needed
1 small green onion, chopped

Directions
Step 1 Heat the sesame oil in a wok or large skillet over medium-high heat, and cook and stir the ginger and garlic before garlic just begins to brown, about 30 seconds. Stir in the pork, breaking it up as you stir, and cook and stir before pork is browned and broken into small pieces. Add the chili bean sauce, soy sauce, sake, and oyster sauce, stir to mix the ingredients together,

reduce heat, and let simmer before mixture thickens slightly, about 3 more minutes.

Step 2 Thin the sauce with water as needed (sauce must not be watery) and gently stir in the tofu. Simmer before tofu is hot and coated with sauce, about 10 minutes, stirring even more times. Serve sprinkled with chopped green onion.

Mild Thai Beef With A Tangerine Sauce

Ingredients

1 (8-ounce) package dry chinese noodles
1/4 cup hoisin sauce
1/4 cup dry sherry
1 teaspoon tangerine zest
1/4 teaspoon ground ginger
4 teaspoons vegetable oil
1 pound flank beef steak, cut diagonally into 2 inch strips
2 teaspoons vegetable oil
1/2 small butternut squash - peeled, seeded, and thinly sliced
1 cup sliced fresh mushrooms
1 large red onion, cut into 2 inch strips
3 cups cabbage, thinly sliced
1 tangerine, sectioned and seeded

Directions

Step 1 Fill a big pot with lightly salted water and bring to a rolling boil over temperature. Following the water is boiling, stir in the noodles, and get back to a boil. Cook the pasta uncovered, stirring occasionally, before pasta has cooked through, but is still firm to the bite, about 5 minutes. Drain, rinse, and reserve.

Step 2 Whisk together the hoisin sauce, sherry, tangerine zest, and ground ginger in just a little bowl.

Step 3 Heat 2 teaspoons vegetable oil in a big wok or skillet over temperature. Add half of the beef slices to the pan; cook, stirring constantly, before meat is nicely browned, 2-3 minutes. Remove meat to a platter with a slotted spoon. Repeat with all of those other beef.

Step 4 Heat all of those other 2 teaspoons of oil in the pan. Stir in the butternut squash, mushrooms, and onion. Cook, stirring constantly, until vegetables are crisp-tender and slightly brown on the edges, 5 to 7 minutes. Add the cabbage, and cook and stir until slightly wilted, about 2 additional minutes.

Step 5 Reduce the heat to medium. Stir the cooked beef, tangerine sections, and hoisin mixture into the vegetables. Cook until heated through, 2-3 minutes. Serve over Chinese noodles.

Moo Goo Gai Pan

Ingredients

1 tablespoon vegetable oil
1 cup sliced fresh mushrooms
2 cups chopped broccoli florets
1 (8-ounce) can sliced bamboo shoots, drained
1 (8-ounce) can sliced water chestnuts, drained
1 (15-ounce) can whole straw mushrooms, drained
1 tablespoon vegetable oil
2 cloves garlic, minced
1 pound skinless, boneless chicken breasts, cut into strips
1 tablespoon cornstarch
1 tablespoon white sugar
1 tablespoon soy sauce
1 tablespoon oyster sauces
1 tablespoon rice wine
1/4 cup chicken broth

Directions

Step 1 Heat 1 tablespoon of vegetable oil in a wok or large skillet over temperature until it begins to smoke. Stir in the brand new mushrooms, broccoli, bamboo shoots, water chestnuts, and straw mushrooms. Cook and stir until all the vegetables are hot, and the broccoli is tender, about 5 minutes. Remove from the wok, and reserve. Get rid of the wok.

Step 2 Heat all of those other tablespoon of vegetable in the wok until it begins to smoke. Stir in the garlic, and cook for a few seconds until it turns golden-brown. Add the chicken, and cook before chicken has lightly browned on the edges, and is forget about pink in the guts, about 5 minutes. Stir together the cornstarch, sugar, soy sauce, oyster sauce, rice wine, and chicken broth in just a little bowl. Pour over the chicken, and bring to a boil, stirring constantly. Boil for about 30 seconds before sauce thickens and is forget about cloudy. Return the vegetables to the wok, and toss with the sauce.

Moo Shu Pork

Ingredients

2 tablespoons soy sauce
1 tablespoon sesame oil
1 tablespoon grated fresh ginger
1 teaspoon minced garlic
3/4 pound pork tenderloin, fat trimmed and pork cut into 1/4-inch strips
2 tablespoons vegetable oil
2 cups shredded napa cabbage
1 carrot, grated
1 pinch salt and ground black pepper to taste

Directions

Step 1 Mix soy sauce, sesame oil, ginger, and garlic in a bowl until marinade is smooth; pour in to a resealable plastic bag. Add pork, coat with the marinade, squeeze out excess air, and seal the bag. Marinate in the refrigerator, 1 hour to overnight.

Step 2 Heat vegetable oil in a wok or large skillet over medium heat. Add cabbage and carrot; cook and stir for you to 2 minutes. Push cabbage mixture aside and add pork with marinade to middle of the skillet. Cook and stir until pork is cooked through, 3 to 4 minutes.

Draw cabbage into the center of the skillet; cook and stir for you to 2 minutes. Season with salt and pepper.

Moo Shu Vegetable Stir Fry

Ingredients

1 tablespoon toasted sesame oils, divided

4 large eggs eggs, lightly beaten

2 cloves garlic, minced

2 teaspoons ground ginger

1 (14-ounce) can bean sprouts, drained

1 (12-ounce) package broccoli slaw

1 tablespoon soy sauce

1 tablespoon rice vinegar

2 tablespoons hoisin sauce

Directions

Step 1 Heat 1 teaspoon sesame oil in a big nonstick skillet over medium heat. Pour in eggs; cook, stirring gently, until set, about 5 minutes. Transfer to a plate.

Step 2 Heat remaining 2 teaspoons oil in the skillet. Add garlic and ginger; cook and stir until fragrant, about 2 minutes. Stir in bean sprouts, broccoli slaw, soy sauce, and rice vinegar; cook until broccoli slaw is tender, about 5 minutes.

Step 3 Stir eggs and hoisin sauce into the skillet until eggs are in small pieces and heated through, around 3 minutes.

Ginger Chicken For Two

Serving: 2 servings. | Prep: 20mins | Cook: 15mins | Ready in:

Ingredients

- 1 egg white, beaten

- 1 tablespoon soy sauce

- 1 teaspoon cornstarch

- 1/8 teaspoon white pepper

- 1/2 pound boneless skinless chicken breasts, cut into 1-inch pieces

- SAUCE:

- 1/4 teaspoon cornstarch

- 1 tablespoon rice vinegar

- 1 tablespoon soy sauce

- 1/2 teaspoon sugar

- STIR-FRY:

- 3 teaspoons peanut or canola oil, divided

- 1/2 medium green pepper, julienned

- 2 green onions, cut into 1-inch lengths

- 1/4 cup canned bamboo shoots, finely chopped

- 1 to 2 teaspoons minced fresh gingerroot

- 3 tablespoons slivered almonds, toasted

- Hot cooked rice, optional

Direction

Mix the soy sauce, pepper, cornstarch, and egg white in a large resealable plastic bag. Place the chicken inside the bag. Seal the bag and flip it until coated. Refrigerate it for 30 minutes. Mix the vinegar, sugar, soy sauce, and cornstarch for the sauce until the mixture is smooth; put aside.

Drain the chicken, discarding its marinade. Stir-fry the chicken in a wok or large skillet with 2 tsp. of oil until the chicken is not anymore pinkish. Remove from the heat and keep it warm.

In the remaining oil, stir-fry the onions and green pepper for 2 minutes. Add the ginger and bamboo shoots. Stir-fry the mixture for 3-4 minutes until the vegetables turn tender-crisp.

Whisk the sauce mixture before pouring it into the pan. Let the mixture boil. Cook for 2 minutes, stirring until thick. Add the chicken and heat the mixture through. Sprinkle the mixture with almonds. Serve the mixture together with the rice, if desired.

Nutrition Information

- Calories: 289 calories

- Fiber: 2g fiber)

- Total Carbohydrate: 9g carbohydrate (3g sugars

- Cholesterol: 63mg cholesterol

- Protein: 30g protein.

- Total Fat: 15g fat (2g saturated fat)

- Sodium: 978mg sodium

Ginger Chicken With Cashews

Serving: 6 | Prep: 25mins | Cook: 15mins | Ready in:
Ingredients

- 1 1/2 cups chicken broth

- 1/2 cup soy sauce

- 1 tablespoon cornstarch

- 3/4 teaspoon ground ginger

- 3/4 teaspoon brown sugar

- 1/4 cup cornstarch

- 1 1/2 teaspoons ground ginger

- 1/4 teaspoon curry powder

- 2 pounds skinless, boneless chicken breast meat
- cut into cubes

- 3 tablespoons extra-virgin olive oil

- 1 tablespoon sesame oil

- 3 green onions, chopped

- 1 bell pepper, chopped

- 1 teaspoon sesame seeds

- 1/2 cup cashews

Direction

- In a small bowl, combine 3/4 teaspoon of ground ginger, chicken broth, brown sugar, 1 tablespoon of cornstarch, and soy sauce.

- In a large, resealable bag, add curry powder, a quarter cup of cornstarch, and 1 1/2 teaspoon of ground ginger. Shake to mix then add chicken. Shake again until chicken pieces are well coated.

- In a large pan or wok set over high heat, heat up sesame oil and olive oil. Cook the chicken for 3 to 5 minutes until golden brown. Mix in bell peppers and green onions, then cook for another 2 to 3 minutes. Add the sauce into the veggie and chicken mixture. Adjust heat to medium. Add in sesame seeds, then allow the mixture to boil for 3 to 5 minutes or until the sauce thickens. Take off from heat. Garnish with cashews then toss before serving.

Nutrition Information

- Calories: 387 calories;

- Sodium: 1359

- Total Carbohydrate: 14.6

- Cholesterol: 92

- Protein: 37.5

- Total Fat: 19.4

CPSIA information can be obtained
at www.ICGtesting.com
Printed in the USA
BVHW051401260522
638205BV00017B/546